W0254265

SNAPSHOTS

SNAPSHOTS

An Album of Essay and Image

Edited by Dinah Lenney

BLOOMSBURY ACADEMIC
LONDON • NEW YORK • OXFORD • NEW DELHI • SYDNEY

BLOOMSBURY ACADEMIC
Bloomsbury Publishing Plc
50 Bedford Square, London, WC1B 3DP, UK
1385 Broadway, New York, NY 10018, USA
29 Earlsfort Terrace, Dublin 2, Ireland

BLOOMSBURY, BLOOMSBURY ACADEMIC and the Diana logo are trademarks of Bloomsbury Publishing Plc

First published in Great Britain 2025

Cover design: Rebecca Heselton
Cover photographs supplied by individual contributors within the book

A catalogue record for this book is available from the British Library.

Library of Congress Cataloging-in-Publication Data

Names: Lenney, Dinah, editor.
Title: Snapshots: an album of essay and image / edited by Dinah Lenney.
Description: London; New York: Bloomsbury Academic, 2025.
Identifiers: LCCN 2024022548 (print) | LCCN 2024022549 (ebook) | ISBN 9781350397057 (hardback) | ISBN 9781350397071 (pdf) | ISBN 9781350397088 (ebook)
Subjects: LCSH: American essays–21st century. | LCGFT: Essays. | Photographs. | Ekphrastic poetry.
Classification: LCC PS689 .S63 2025 (print) | LCC PS689 (ebook) | DDC 814/.608—dc23/eng/20240605
LC record available at https://lccn.loc.gov/2024022548
LC ebook record available at https://lccn.loc.gov/2024022549

ISBN: HB: 978-1-3503-9705-7
ePDF: 978-1-3503-9707-1
eBook: 978-1-3503-9708-8

Typeset by RefineCatch Limited, Bungay, Suffolk
Printed and bound in Great Britain

To find out more about our authors and books visit www.bloomsbury.com and sign up for our newsletters.

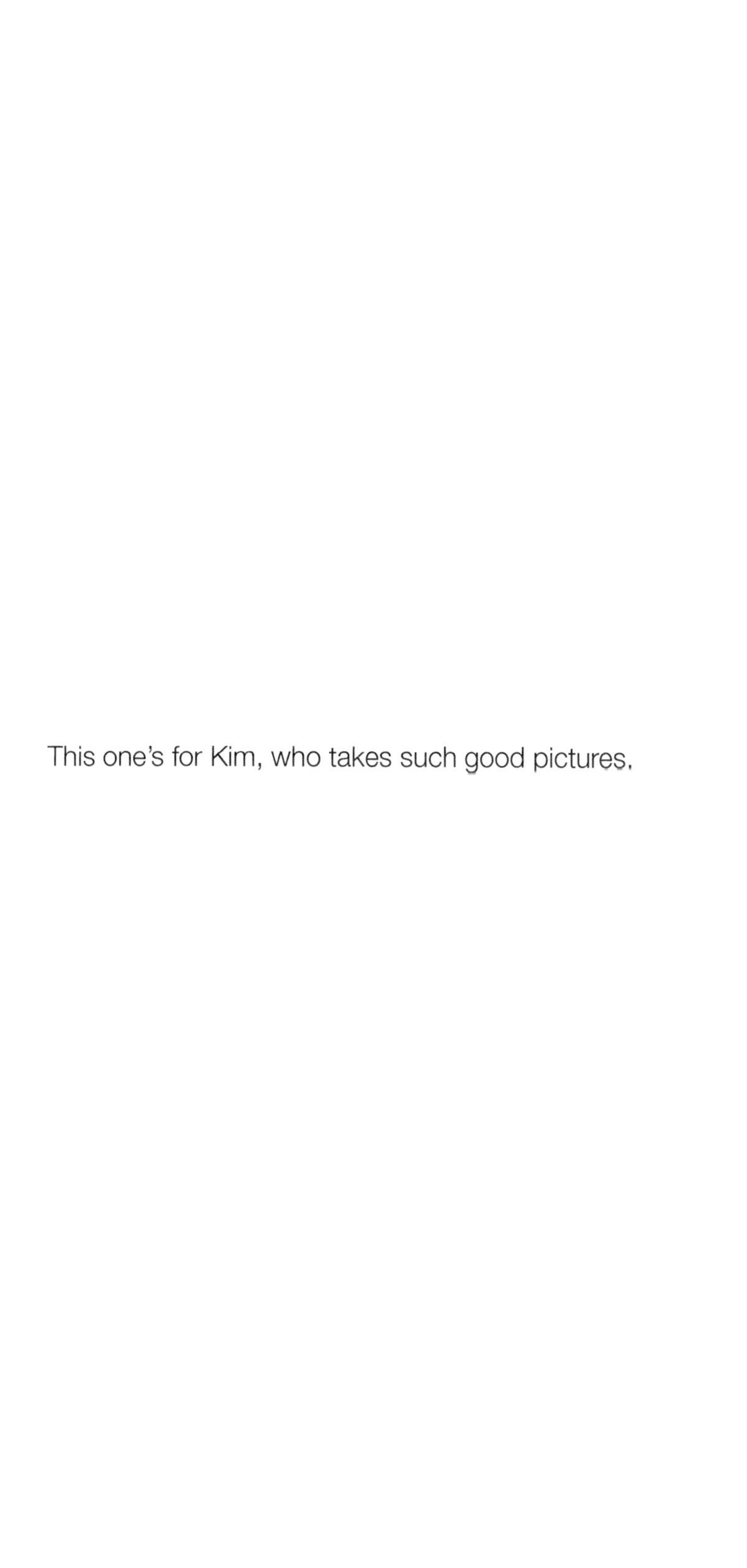

This one's for Kim, who takes such good pictures.

A Drinking Song

Wine comes in at the mouth
And love comes in at the eye;
That's all we shall know for truth
Before we grow old and die.
I lift the glass to my mouth,
I look at you, and I sigh.

WILLIAM BUTLER YEATS

CONTENTS

*

POSTSCRIPT

ACKNOWLEDGMENTS

First, thanks to these gifted and generous contributors for permitting me to share their words and their pictures.

Grateful, also, to Amy Gerstler, Susan Scarf Merrell, Rachel Pastan, Kitty Swink, and the Yale Women of LA Writers Group for spurring me on; to Jane Lancillotti for last minute inspiration; and to artist/designer Gail Swanlund for her beautiful work throughout—

And to Fred for patience (and fortitude) and making me laugh, to Eliza and Jake, who are never not willing to sort me out, and to Lucy Brown, Aanchal Vij, David Campbell, and everyone at Bloomsbury, for bringing us all together in one beautiful book.

DINAH LENNEY

INTRODUCTION: A PICTURE *IS* WORTH A THOUSAND WORDS

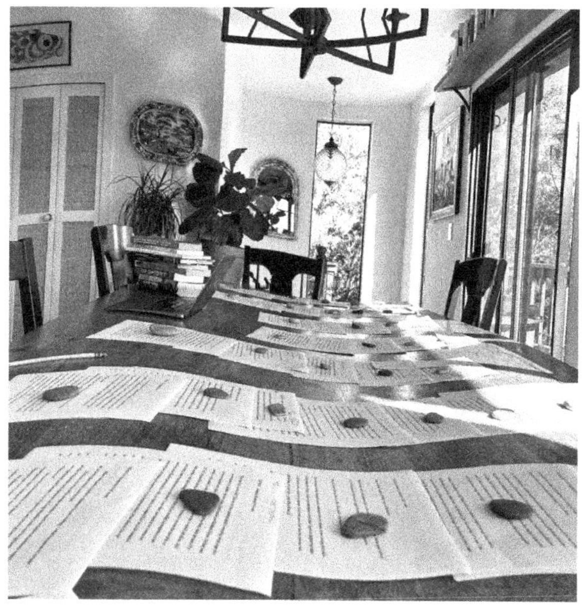

"Something new is going on out there."

That's how the editors introduced *In Short,* the first of the late Judith Kitchen's four anthologies of brief literary nonfiction. Then, a bit further down, "Like many another new thing," they wrote, "the Short is in some ways not really new." That was three decades go. By the time Judith and I worked together on *Brief Encounters*, her last in the series, short nonfiction had become a regular feature of journals, collections, and course syllabi world over.

Even so, with *Snapshots*, my follow-up of sorts to the previous four books, I want to make that same claim: *Something new is going on out there.* But I, too, should qualify; yes, I'm adding an element this time: photographs. And yet. Ekphrasis goes at least as far back as Homer's description of Achilles' shield in *The Iliad* (800 B.C.). The Poetry Foundation defines the device like so: "Through the imaginative act of narrating and reflecting on the 'action' of a painting or sculpture, the poet may amplify and expand its meaning."

And here's an extended definition from *The Penguin Dictionary of Literary Terms and Literary Theory* (borrowed from contributor Amy Gerstler):

Ekphrasis/ecphrasis: The intense pictorial description of an object. This very broad term has been limited by some to the description of art-objects [. . .] A more generous account would define *ekphrasis* as virtuosic description of physical reality (objects, scenes, persons) in order to evoke an image in the mind's eye as intense as if the described object were actually before the reader.

And already I'm balking—why this big word for something writers just naturally do, with art, certainly; but also, see above, with music, dance, food, flowers, funerals, weddings, holidays, and all manner of experience and event. If it's true that any of these move us to think and feel and remember, to interrogate the reasons for our personal associations, why the label? The answer, I suppose, has originally to do with *visual* inspiration—the challenge of making art about art—and photos, some of them at least, certainly qualify. But ekphrasis, from the Greek, translates simply to "description." Which is not what I was after in this collection of essays; not that description doesn't show up; not that describing isn't worth doing. But first, find me a piece herein that *only* describes the photo that prompted it. And second, as Judith Kitchen writes in *Half in Shade*, her own collected collage of memoir and conjecture in response to a box of old family photos, "snapshots [. . .] are somewhat exempt from 'artistic scrutiny.'" Third, in the case of these 36 essays, the "image in the mind's eye" is intense because "the objects"—the pictures that ignited the prose—*are* "actually before the reader."

So the more I think about ekphrasis in relation to this project, the more I want to push back. Take for instance, a seminal paper, "Ekphrasis and the Still Movement of Poetry," first published in 1967 by renowned critic and theorist Murray Krieger, in which he states that ekphrasis, as a critical device, is an attempt to recreate the *stillness* of fine art in words; further, he implies this is a nearly impossible task, since words, like music, cannot be stilled. True enough, yet I find myself itching to quibble: Do poets—do writers of any genre—aim to emulate stillness? Or do we strive to make something that breathes? Even sings? And isn't it wonderful to consider this strange and naturally occurring symbiosis? That a painter or sculptor—especially a photographer—might intend to freeze time, only for the poet or writer who encounters that frozen moment to feel compelled to get it ticking again? That's what the writers in *Snapshots* have done: In illuminating the events, relationships, people, and places captured in their photos they have given those images new meaning and resonance—new life.

But I digress—and maybe I protest too much—if these essays are ekphrastic (and they are, of course), they follow in a long tradition. Nor is writing specifically about photographs a novel idea. *Let Us Now Praise Famous Men*—James Agee's collaboration with Walker Evans, a study of post-Great Depression poverty in the American South—was first published in 1941; Susan Sontag's *On Photography*, a collection of essays about the art and politics of taking pictures, has been in print since 1977; Roland Barthes's form-breaking, genre-defying *Camera Lucida* appeared in 1980. Off the top of my head, in no particular order, just a few famous examples of the similarly preoccupied: W. G. Sebald in four genre-bending novels; memoirists Sally Mann, Patti Smith, Annie Ernaux, and Jennifer Croft; journalists and essayists Janet Malcolm, Geoff Dyer, Teju Cole, Lynell George, Jeff Sharlet, and Judith Kitchen (as noted). And that's the tip of the berg.

However—the caveat being that things get old pretty quickly these days—social media has changed up the game. So what's new-*ish*, anyway, is daily self-publishing, and not just words; not just politics and self-promotion and #mondaymotivations and #thursdaythoughts, but, more often than not, companion photographs. I'm not the first to wonder why we're baring our souls (kitchens, bedrooms, closets, and drawers) to strangers; nor the first to exult in my phone's capabilities; nor have I been able myself to resist all this snapping and posting. But even as I fall in line, I can't help but wonder: Why this compulsion to illustrate our days?

Mostly, I'd say, it's because we can. Because it's easy and instantly gratifying not only to publicly revel or wallow in our personal news, tastes, vanities, loves, and losses, but to put them on display. And my plan, in conceiving of a follow-up collection of nonfiction shorts, was to reflect the trend. But the thing about plans—they get away from us, don't they? Iris Murdoch is known to have said that "every book is the wreck of a perfect idea." Meaning, of course, there's no such thing; suggesting that any project worth doing takes on a life of its own.

I did start on task: I mostly solicited work from writers who like to take pictures. I asked each of them to choose a personal photo, black and white, as a prompt to write something/anything short and nonfictional, please. Otherwise, the assignment was broad. The guidelines didn't reflect my own iPhone obsession: I didn't insist my writers take the photo, nor did I restrict them to recent experience. The task—regardless of who hit the shutter or when—was to write *from* or *into* the image; not so much to describe, as to enter the frame and/or to think beyond its borders: What sorts of memories, feelings, revelations might emerge?

And the outcome: Several of these essays wind up mirroring the way we live now, but many do not. The collection turns out to be more various than I might have anticipated—less of this particular cultural moment than it is universal and timeless, somehow, in its subjects and themes. Singly and together, these pieces span great swaths of geography and experience. They testify less to the urge to document our every move, than to a powerful desire to remember, understand, grieve, forgive, celebrate, honor, love, and finally *move on*. Rich and diverse in style and tone, they prove my thesis: A picture is worth as many words in as many keys as we please; and how powerful the sound of all these voices rising up from one place.

A few words about my attempt to orchestrate: Practically speaking, the day came when I finally spread the essays, all 36 of them, across my big kitchen table. I took a photo, and posted, of course (using a filter called "Wave" to demonstrate the dizzying business before me). Since the windows were open and the morning was breezy, I'd weighed down each piece with a stone. Said a friend in the comments under my post: *The rocks are a nice touch.* I explained about keeping the pages from blowing away. *Of course!* she replied. *But they look magically like a trail to follow through the story.*

Yes, I thought, good. But what was the story exactly? How should it unfold? It seemed obvious to categorize somehow, but under what headings? Past, Present, Future? Travel and Work? Beginnings and Endings? People and Things?

Immediately obvious was that Major Jackson's prose poem—which muses on inspiration itself—should start us off. And that Abigail Thomas's "Piggies"—about what to do when inspiration fails—was the perfect way to close. For the rest: I finally decided on seven sections. But I might have come up with seven others. And as pleased as I am with where each essay lands, they could have settled elsewhere, it's true. Just for instance, Suzanne Berne's "Celebration" is as much about the power of art as it is about her grandfather; and Brandon Shimoda's "Yamato" is as much about his grandfather as it is about the power of art. Both Alex Espinoza and Dinty W. Moore turn the lens on themselves when we least expect it. Same deal with David L. Ulin's "Wild Turkey": Though I've placed it elsewhere, as with Alex and Dinty's literary "selfies," it might have happily lived in the section I've called 'Mirror, Mirror.'

Which reminds me: Photographer Ralph Steiner is quoted as having said that every photo *is* a self-portrait. The same might be said of these essays, infused as they are with personal insight—with wishing, reckoning, accepting—each one with its image, intimately and generously revealing of the writer who placed them side by side.

What I also found was that every essay, however brief, is abundantly, intricately layered, all of them together presenting a multitude of angles to consider and dots to connect; with that in mind I hope you'll consult the appendix of recurring themes at the end of the collection. Also, I've included a short list of recommended reading, and a long list of writing prompts to add to your arsenals. And to keep in mind: As is true of all prompts, as is evidenced by the variety of strategies and structures here—from straight ahead memoir, to profile, to creative manifesto, to cultural commentary, to family history, to confession, to eulogy, to real-time conversation—there's no right or wrong way to approach. Whatever we decide to call the exercise, ekphrasis or free write (or anything and everything in between), you don't have to be poet or a critic to be sparked by a photo. You don't have to be a photographer either. You don't have to know anything about the art or craft. You only have to try to discover what an image means to you: How does it remind you? Comfort or disturb you? Bring you closer to the truth of what you think and who you are?

Would it help to know something more about the medium? I guess it could. Might that same knowledge get in your way? Not if you don't let it.

For our purposes, though, unless expertise makes a difference to you, it makes none at all to your reader. As with all personal writing, it's you, even more than your subject, we're hoping to get to know; if that's not why we first come to the page, it's certainly the reason we stay. That's what I discovered wherever, however I followed the stones. That's the story. *Snapshots* is a testament to our human desire to figure out how we're connected—to place, history, memory, future and past—and to know and be known to each other here and now.

—Dinah Lenney

PROLOGUE

MAJOR JACKSON
Emerson Motor Works
Rochester, Vermont

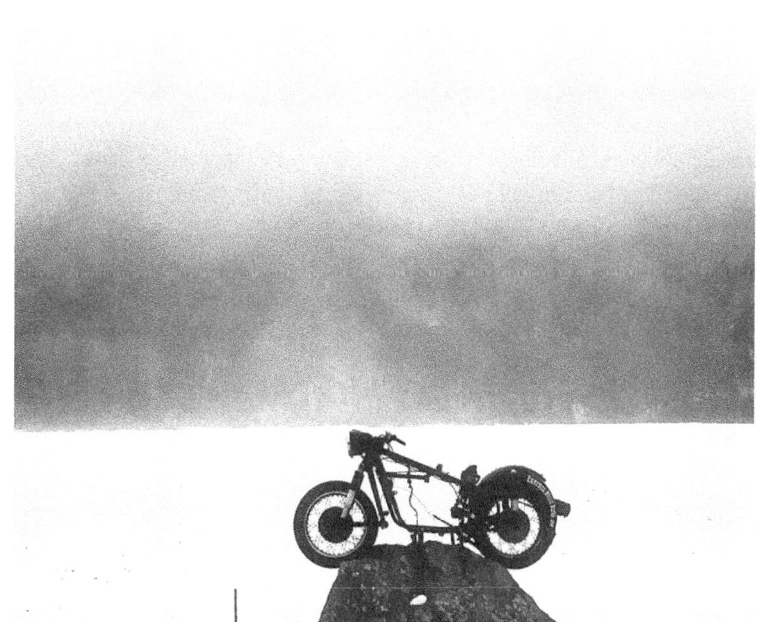

What prepares us for the possible, a conveyance through the silent mist, as when one imagines mounting a riderless motorbike dropped from a cloud last seen on the frontlines of the Kasserine Pass and commanded by the Bersaglieri whose helmeted plumage of black capercaillie feathers put you in mind of an aggravated grouse? No showtunes are to be found here. All ideas and saviors dissipate in a spiraling haze of white, especially the troubadours who traded in citherns for gunnery, deceived by the interior designs of trenches. Your loneliness contains an analogue; it is displayed on a boulder on the side of a road in Rochester, Vermont. Driving speedily past one morning along Route 100, aroused, you caught a glimpse and were changed forever by its whimsy like an ultrasound in the body. Rubbernecking at the speed of sound, lightening-like: rubber tires and a spot of snow making a disappointed though friendly face. Does all perception arrive at a rate of velocity reminiscent of a falling star or is the work of *Imagism* more a slow melting that reveals dark soil awaiting an alluvial mind? Above the prairie, that is no longer a prairie but a snowfield, imagine Vermeer's cornflower blue, his canvas of the pearl-earringed girl, her lips of glossy red opening like an homage to awe. Emerson wrote "And now my chains are to be broken; I shall mount about these clouds and opaque airs in which I live [...] comprehend my relations. That will reconcile me to life, and renovate nature, to see trifles animated by a tendency, and to know what I am doing. Life will no more be a noise."

1 WAY BACK WHEN

"The future waits for you."

NAOMI SHIHAB NYE

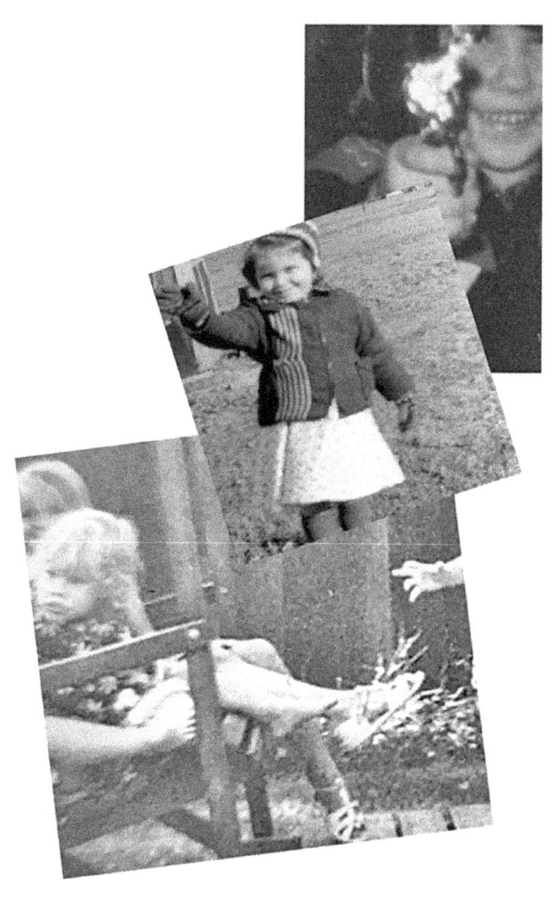

SONJA LIVINGSTON
VIGILANTE

Here's the gunslinger. Here's the outlaw, the bandit, the pistol-wielding desperado. Here's the die-cast six shooter with a bird etched into the barrel and the star of Texas on the grip.

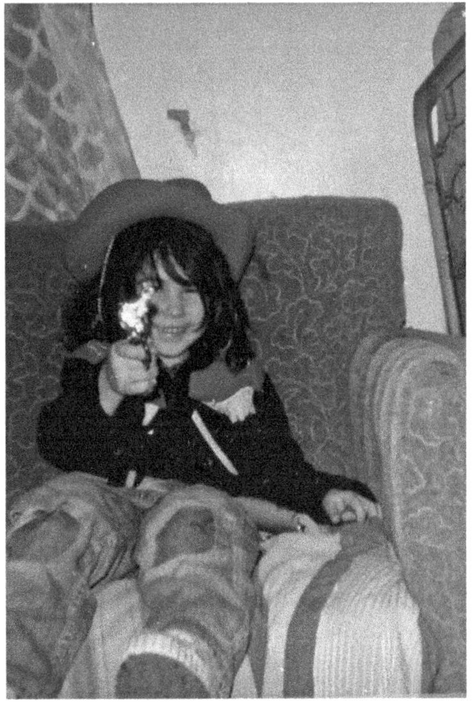

Here's the fringed shirt and plastic holster stretched across her lap. Here's the hammer drawing back and the cap waiting to explode. Here's my sister squinting her left eye and pulling the trigger the exact second she's told to smile.

Here's our brother's cast-off jeans. Here's knees so worn, the patches barely hold. Here's a chair with scuffed velvet leaves and a stain shaped like the state of Florida overhead. Here's tar shingles and cracked linoleum floors. Here's Leighton Avenue, Bowman, and East Main Street, upper and lower. Here's a thousand moves and never getting anywhere.

Here's food baskets at Christmas and my mother and all her children streaming downtown for a summer parade. Here's the man selling balloons and fireworks overhead. Here's my sister peeling off her shirt and flying outside with snarls in her hair. Here's rejecting catechism and the gilded harness of Mass. Here's the solidity of bread from the corner store versus a shimmering mystery which may or may not appear.

Here's trying to lasso our flickering shapeshifting mother and scouting fathers on TV. Here's reruns of *Baretta, Bonanza* and *The Wild Wild West.* Here's the six o'clock news reporting a body out by the highway and another missing girl. Here's grown men slowing their cars to watch us play and older boys standing so close the tang of sweat gets in our nose. Here's underprotected and overexposed. Here's a thousand shots compressed onto paper strips. Here's losing your gun and using rocks to strike the caps one at a time. Here's a\\the whiff of smoke and the satisfying *pop.* Here's sparks encircling our heads. Here's the moment the body becomes a shield.

Here's the sister who makes lists and shops when her mother cannot. Here's men swaddling liquor bottles in broad daylight. Here's boxes of mac and cheese and cool jugs of milk. Here's *Now and Laters, Chick-O-Sticks* and *RedHots.* Here's the shame of food stamps and the child brave enough to use them. Here's rescuing strays from the back lot. Here's letting the momma cat give birth in her dresser drawer and the kittens' mewling faces. Here's staying up all night with the runt. Here's scrounging money for medicine and ferrying them to some other street when our mother says *there's not enough for seven kids let alone felines.*

Here's an army man strapped to a square of silken cloth. Here's throwing him high into the air and watching him parachute back to earth. Here's the durability of tiny metal figures. Here's an oath against weakness and kicking Michael Pusateri's ass in the #33 School parking lot. Here's adding a steering wheel to a stolen shopping cart and piecing together a bicycle from scavenged pieces. Here's forward motion when everything around you is still.

Here's *Hide and Seek, Freeze Tag* and *Chase*. Here's making a homemade *Monopoly* game. Here's staying up late, trying to remember the names of properties from some other kid's board. Here's a dark-haired girl wiping sleep from her eyes while cutting out *Get Out of Jail Free!* cards.

Here's piling into bed with her sisters and the crack in the plaster wall becoming lightning with every passing car. Here's tunneling under the covers and flapping blankets to make electricity in the dark. Here's sparklers without powder, flashes without smoke. Here's radiance where you least expect it and falling asleep with heads full of light.

Here's the impossibility of keeping the splinters and barbs of the world at bay no matter how we arm ourselves. Here's the exhaustion of standing at attention and how fast the decades pass. Here's asking, after all these years, whether we might be able to put these old weapons away?

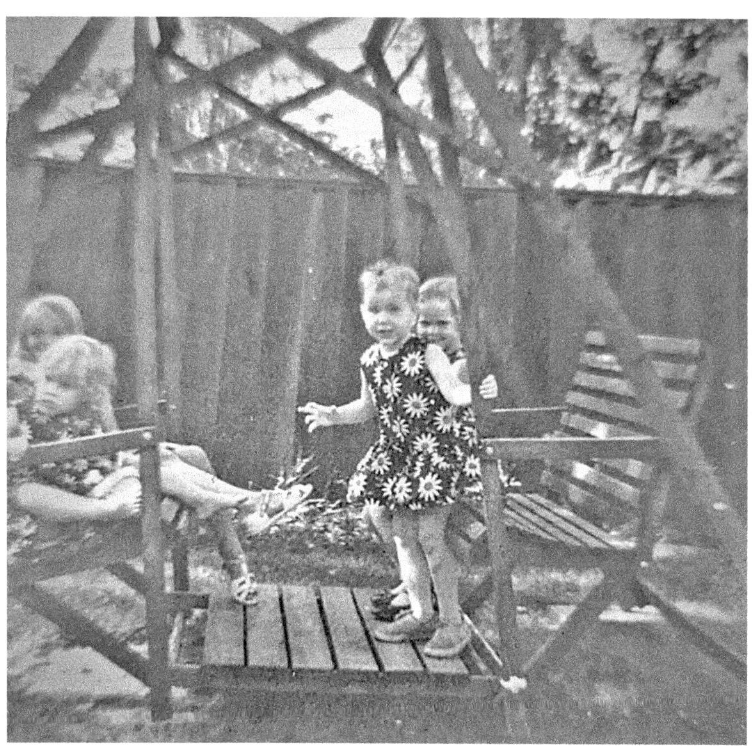

KATE CARROLL DE GUTES
GIRL BY DEFAULT

Four blonde girls. Wavy tresses cascade to the shoulders of two of them. They wear white gloves not visible in this photo. One is outfitted in impossibly white sandals. The other girl's spotless white knee socks slouch towards her ankles and her black, patent leather Mary Janes. The youngest child sits barefoot on the glider where some mother or grandmother or aunt has posed all four for the photo labeled on the back in blue ink, July 4, 1968.

The girl who looks straight at the camera has hair not much longer than it will be 55 years later when—every four weeks—she gets a "nonbinary cut with clippers" at the queer barbershop within walking distance of her house. She is girl by default. Girl by the fact of her dress (which matches the other three) and the bow taped into her hair by her mother. There is no mistaking this child's gender.

Her PF Flyers, designed to help kids "run faster and jump higher"—once white canvas—look grey in this photo. On this day, no white anklets trimmed in lace, favored by the girl's mother. For some reason, her mother has tied the damp shoes onto bare feet, sparking right then a lifelong aversion to shoes without socks.

*

I remember feeling the bottoms of my feet pruning up in those shoes, remember the stifling humidity that exacerbated the discomfort between my toes. Worst of all, I remember the fabric of the matching navy-blue dress. The complex, textured structure of the twill actually made it stiffer even than the shoes I wore; my three-and-a-half year-old self felt how heavy it was the moment my mother pulled the dress over my head. The bodice chafed the delicate skin at the front of my armpits and rubbed raw my tiny nipples. The flared skirt spread around me when I finally sat on the glider, but then my legs stuck to the varnished slats.

*

My wife calls me her "special snowflake." So many environmental factors affect me: Scented laundry detergent makes me sneeze and causes an immediate headache; soy products bloat my belly and lead to uncontrollable gas; air "fresheners" swell my eyes shut and trigger wheezing and whining. Gluten pimples my arms in tiny white bumps and creates some internal chemical brew resulting in weird body odor. Starch produces hives bordering on welts wherever it touches me. My sensitive system struggles.

*

I'm projecting, I know, when I look at this picture. I see a child who wants to jump off and out of the frame. A kid who had begged her mother—10, 20, maybe 30 minutes earlier—to be excused from wearing the horrible dress. That it matched the others only added to my misery, I'm sure. But that might simply be more projection.

What I know for certain is that even at three-and-a-half, this outfit didn't square with my self-image. So, though a slight smile plays across that tiny face, even though my eyes are bright and engaged with the photographer, I believe that child wanted to return to wherever it was that left the mud stains on her knees and shins.

Why didn't my mother wash off my legs? Perhaps she cared less than I remember that her first born mostly refused to dress like other girls, preferred to play alone rather than with girls in white gloves. My mother had a great ability to let kids be kids—up to a point, age seven or so. Then she expected me to follow social cues, expected me to conform, even purchased Candies shoes and a sleeveless aqua polyester dress for my junior high graduation. She left me to figure out how to ascend and descend the stage stairs in backless, three-inch heels.

*

In a second photo taken a moment before or a moment after this one, the pre-schooler sits in the middle of the bench, her arm casually reaching out to the arm of the glider. Self-contained amid the girly chaos. Head cocked to the right side even then, considering what? Perhaps the twill and canvas in her future. Carhartt chore coats and logger jeans. White canvas Jack Purcell sneakers, so much more butch than the daintily tapered PF Flyers in the picture. Nine years later her father will take her back-to-school shopping at The Children's Bootery in downtown Novato, California, and buy her a 1970s-style pair of navy-blue Keds with red and orange stripes racing across the toes. Very obviously a boy's shoe. But her father won't argue when she picks them out; he'll just ask the store owner to make sure they fit correctly.

Later that day her mother puts the sneakers—still in their box—on the top shelf of the girl's closet. It doesn't occur to the girl that her mother means to return them. Before she can, the about-to-be-fourth-grader puts them on and sneaks out of the house and down to the creek. Careful, she believes, not to get the white rubber edges of the shoes dirty.

But once home, she sees her mistake. Even soap and water can't remove the ochre dust of a California summer. She takes care as she wraps the shoes in their tissue and puts them back on the shelf in her closet. She forgets about them. Forgets until her mother takes down the box and inspects them, no longer new. Fury fills her mother's brown eyes. The Keds cannot be returned. Her mother doesn't say this. Instead she says, *well, you'll just have to wear dirty shoes on the first day of school.*

That's okay. At least they're the right shoes. And the girl wears them almost every day for the rest of the year. With socks. The comfortable kind, not those stretchy ones with the lace.

NAOMI SHIHAB NYE
GOODBYE TO EVERYTHING AND EVERYBODY

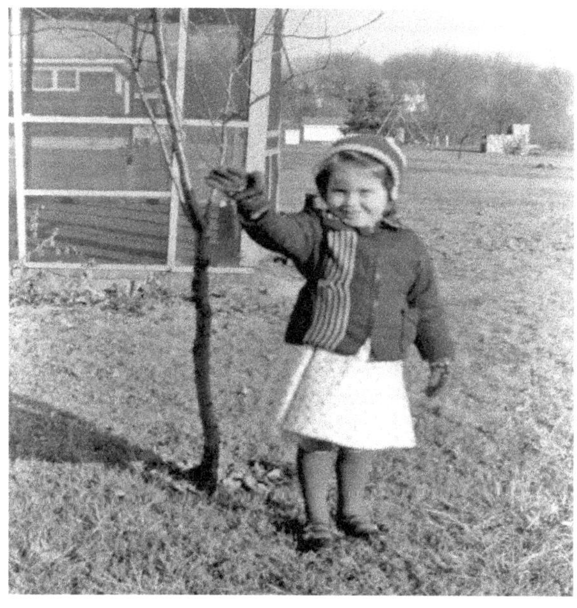

They thought I was waving hello, but no. Walking out by myself into gray skies, gray streets, an enormous cloud of nostalgia surrounding me every waking moment, an almost intolerable sense that everything was vanishing even as we witnessed it. No one talked about this. You could smell the river even from a distance. It colored us all. White petals curling on our two skinny cherry trees would not be in blossom long. I walked to school by myself from the age of six on. Now that seems impossible. How were we so confident? Getting to school involved crossing a creek, climbing a hill, various turns. I always made it there and home again, only once attacked by a never-before-seen dog who leapt up and bit me on the cheek, under the eye, for no reason. Stitches—but no scar. Young skin heals. After that strange encounter, they still let me go alone. Sometimes I'd catch up with another girl or two, and we'd pick our favorite houses out on any block. I liked the one with no paint because it seemed sad. Always that sense of disappearing, being temporary on the earth, always afraid my mother might dissolve in my absence. How could I have known she would be with me till she was 94? She was so thin, translucent sometimes, full of tears, more tears than a baby—what was she always crying for? No one told me. Sometimes she didn't even seem to know. Her shiny ponytail... from the back she looked happy. We lived in the cradle of mystery, but it felt exquisite. Under my bed, shoe boxes of scrappy papers, lines about cities and squirrels, tiny prayers for everyone. We raised our hands to our lives, welcoming them in. We waved goodbye when we had to, and I knew I was waving goodbye every single day. What was coming next? What was wrong with me? I did not want to grow up even for a minute. When people talked about future ambitions, what they dreamed of being, I turned my head away. In order to reach any future, we would have to say goodbye to a blue bowl of oatmeal made by someone else, placed on the table next to one small silver spoon. Folded laundry on the bed quietly welcoming us home from school. Saturday story hour at the library, where Robert Louis Stevenson and Margaret Wise Brown were still alive telling us dreamy things we wanted to hear more than once. I'd think—I'm not giving this up. I don't want to be in the front seat. I don't want a bank account, a driver's license. My quarters lived in a striped sock with holes, tucked into the drawer. No one would find them. Go on without me. The future waits for you. Give me open screens at night, breeze waffling through, enormous pine trees, lines of tulips in the yard. My grandmother rang us up just to say hello, but otherwise that little black telephone on its shrine in the hallway cubbyhole rarely jangled. No one needed us, I didn't need them either. Mostly Grandma and I rode buses downtown, dining in department stores, Famous & Barr, Stix, Baer & Fuller. She bought me luscious eclairs and chocolate pie with whipped cream if I wanted it, something my mother would never have done. Once I saw a doll as big as I was and asked for it. At Christmas when my grandma turned up lugging that oversized smiling doll wearing clothes, with gleaming eyes and bangs, my mother glared at me. She knew I must have asked for it. Where did she ever go? Next year Grandma brought me a guitar. I received few other messages except from fences and gates, green yards, tangled bushes, acorns, twigs and clouds drifting silently above, echoing the river, and the pavement. We were in the center. Of the country, the world, our lives. But how could childhood be the center? You had to be grown-up longer than you got to be a child. This did not feel fair. No one had heard of Ferguson except people who lived there or next door in Florissant or Cool Valley. Some people in downtown St. Louis had never even been to Ferguson. I knew people who lived in Kinloch right beside us and wondered why we didn't get to be together. Later that would change and Ferguson would become famous for sad reasons. Who knew? Who could ever guess? We were invisible and we liked it. I was afraid of tornadoes, water towers, spiders. I knew a girl who said she couldn't wait to grow up because then she'd be free. I stared at her. Are you kidding? We're free now. Don't you feel how free we are? When I thought about being older, it felt like doom, separation, struggle, loss of empty hours, grief, crying, painful knees like my grandma had, tight black shoes, no running through a vacant lot, no muddy hours, no secret cookies from Grandma's closet. And people would die. So many people. And you might have to live longer without them. How could anyone stand it? Fifty years later, one friend from our block would round us up again. Eight of us. We would sit in a circle in our same old field. Still empty. Tall grasses still waving. What was the secret in your house? he asked. One said, my parents never stopped drinking. Another, my brother used to lock me in the closet. I said, my mother cried all the time, I tried to hide it from you. They only remembered her smiling. What I couldn't say—I loved our lives too much. We were there together. Close to the ground. We knew things. The precious tender threadbare glory of each day. And my heart was broken broken broken because, like the worst loser-Buddhist there could ever be, I wanted it to stay.

2 FAMILY PORTRAITS

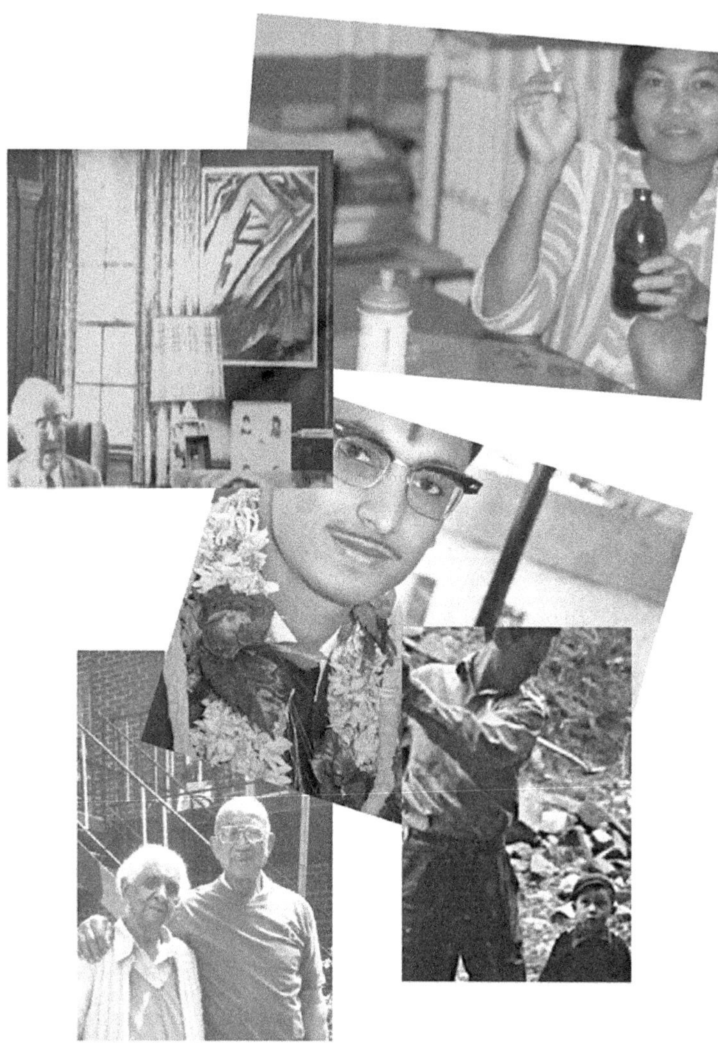

"In the way of children, I thought—because I didn't think—that my grandmother had always been as she was."

CLIFFORD THOMPSON

GRACE TALUSAN
FREEDOM

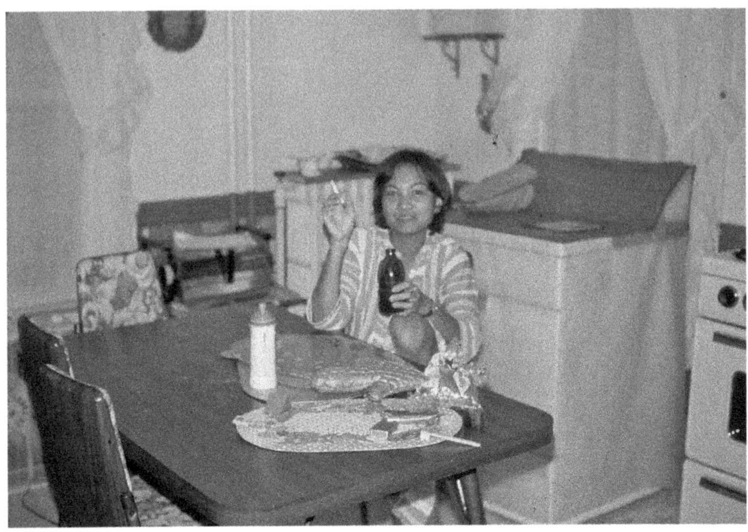

My mother sits with one bare foot on the chair; her knee becomes an armrest, her shin touching the table where her family eats breakfast, a cigarette in one hand, a beer in the other. It's a warm evening in 1977 back when we lived on the top floor of a triple decker in Boston. She is 30 years old.

So far she has three children—disappointments for being born daughters—and her husband wants to keep trying until they get sons. Years from now, they will have two, and at first, the boys will solve their problem of unhappiness—until even they fail to make their parents happy.

On this night I am five and asleep by the time my father sneaks out of the bedroom where he's studying and points the lens at my mother. Still, I can see him saying, "Caught you," as he laughs for getting away with something. He taunts her, threatening, "Now your family will see how America has changed you. What are you, a women's libber? A feminist?"

After two years in America, my mother is different. She is finally out of sight of her mother, her elderly *titas*, her older *ates*, and all the women who enforce womanhood. She is out of the whisper range of the helpers who are always listening and currying favor by reporting their observations to her mother. Even God himself, at least the Catholic one that the Spanish colonizers brought to the Philippines, has been left behind in the Philippines. In America, for the first time in her life, she is free.

And yet, she's bone tired, doing things that she's never had to do before: scrubbing floors and toilets, shopping and cooking, her fingers chapped and cracking from detergents and soaps, the constant washing of her hands after changing the baby's diapers. Back home, a single person did a single job. Back home, each house was alive with *kasambahay*: the *lavandera*, the cook, the housemaids, and at least one *yaya* per child.

In the States, my mother is all alone with all the jobs. Free to be alone with her aloneness.

She hasn't yet given up the idea of working professionally. After all, she's studied her whole life towards becoming a doctor. If the babysitter shows up, she rides the Orange line to work at a lab. She's not sure if she should trust the women she hires (and eventually fires), these unsupervised strangers, to care for her babies. Back home, her mother managed the *kasambahay* because someone needed to watch the watchers.

When her five kids are in high school and college, my mother finds out she's a published author in multiple science papers. She worked in a research lab before she decided she could not be both in this country, a mother and a physician, and it turns out that the supervising doctor included her name on the studies she contributed to; but she finds out long after anyone remembers that she had been a doctor once, too. In the Philippines, she was a radiologist. But in America, she is a cook, a driver, a bank machine, a permission giver; her children's mother and her husband's wife.

In the photo, at 30, she is young enough for her body to remain thin after the pregnancies. She is on the cusp of her adult life. Except for the recent loss of her father, when she first kissed grief, she's still too early in her life to know the worst pain ahead. Abandonment, betrayal, loneliness, despair. The common stuff.

Her face is unlined and unworried. Her babies are finally asleep. The littlest one took most of her bottle; the two older ones brushed their teeth. The tiny plastic toys that get underfoot are picked up. The appliances are wiped clean and protected with dust covers until tomorrow when she'll sacrifice again, doing the work of house helpers, and, for the sake of the family, help her husband pass the exam for foreign medical school graduates. If he doesn't pass, they will have to go home.

But which place is home? She can't believe she feels this way after only two years. Everything she loved is on the other side of the world, but the truth is that she doesn't want to return. This version of herself would never be happy back there. That self always agreed with her mother and did whatever the Church asked. This self talks back to her husband; she asks for what she wants. And what she wants is the freedom to find out who she will become.

Before she settles down to relax at the breakfast table, she even slips a cigarette from his pack and fishes one of his beers from the vegetable crisper. She's never drunk a soda, much less a beer, straight from the bottle before. Her mother taught her that "a lady only drinks from a drinking glass, never a bottle or a straw," but her mother isn't here to warn her about all the ways to avoid becoming a slut, a sinner, a ruined woman.

Anyway, it's already too late.

AIMEE LIU
AXED

You two! Stop! You're breaking my heart, and you don't even know me yet.

Father, won't you lay down your axe and *look* at that little doppelganger? He's still so hungry and so young. I'd give anything to shake you both together to wake to this magic, this flicker of light and all those damp stones ripe for the stacking, the delicious crunch of fall's betweenness; sweater weather despite your shirtsleeves (oh, how that boy wishes you'd invite him to strip down beside you). Hear the mutter of old crows circling? Surely you can smell the bright threads of smoke warning you have no time to lose.

One quivering tendril remains. It's only mine anymore. And yet, I persist.

Put down that axe, Dad, won't you please? I know you think you're hoisting a world of woes, debts and losses incurred for what you can't be sure. This land you're clearing. The house you'll build. A place in the woods. A family, a home. The good capable husband/provider, your pose of a lifetime.

You hardly knew your own distant father. The family's resident foreigner. Who else could you be?

Oh yes, you've got your excuses. Except really, they've got you. No matter how hard you pretend to have them all in hand, those masculine doubts and insecurities work away in plain view. We can see them even now consuming, hollowing you from the inside out until nothing's left but the darkness that your little boy ventures to touch.

Show me, he begs. *Let me help.* He thinks, *I just want to be like you.*

The way he mirrors you there in the woods, his little legs wide like yours, his insatiable eyes and ears and heart. Your child wants nothing more than a glance, a word, permission to come close. Take hold of this moment! This fissure in time, this crack in the past still offers just enough light for you to escape the never-ever understanding. All you need is to face him.

But you can't find your own way out, let alone let him in.

Get back, your shadow growls. *You're going to get hurt. Go stand with your mother.*

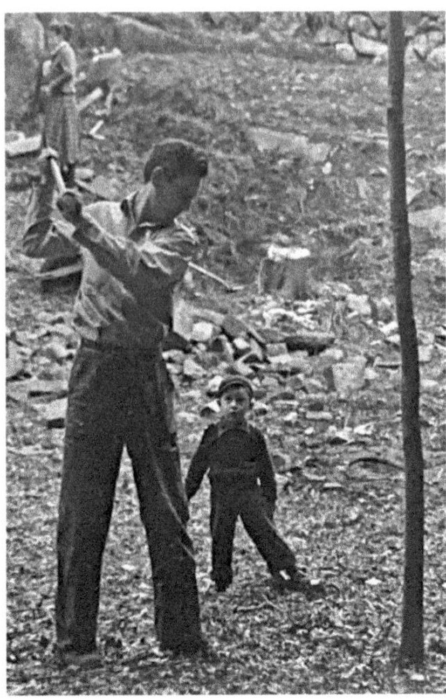

There, in the tattersall skirt. See her in the background, right behind the raised axe? The mother who trussed her little boy up in that too-adorable jacket and cap, which she forbids him to shed. The wife behind your phantom house. The heart of your misgivings.

Even at three, your son knows this mother is no substitute. But how can he explain? He's only three, and you're the father.

You're the one holding the axe.

I'm trying to warn you his time will come. He won't "get back." He will not yield. Instead, he'll seek and then revere men who show him not just how to brandish his blade but how to swing it hard. Other men, I mean.

I'll be around to witness that. And so will you.

For now, though, my little big brother stares, gulping the potent scent of you years before I'm born. Before I take my own stubborn turn, his sister, your daughter, aping your silence and yearning, too, to touch the you inside that darkness.

The next frames are lost, but I'll tell you what you'd see if they weren't: the long, mute arc of that damned axe. Ever slicing downward.

Such tenacious saplings, your targets, yet you hardly even see them.

SEJAL SHAH
SERPENTINE

For my father, Ashok N. Shah (1939–2023)*

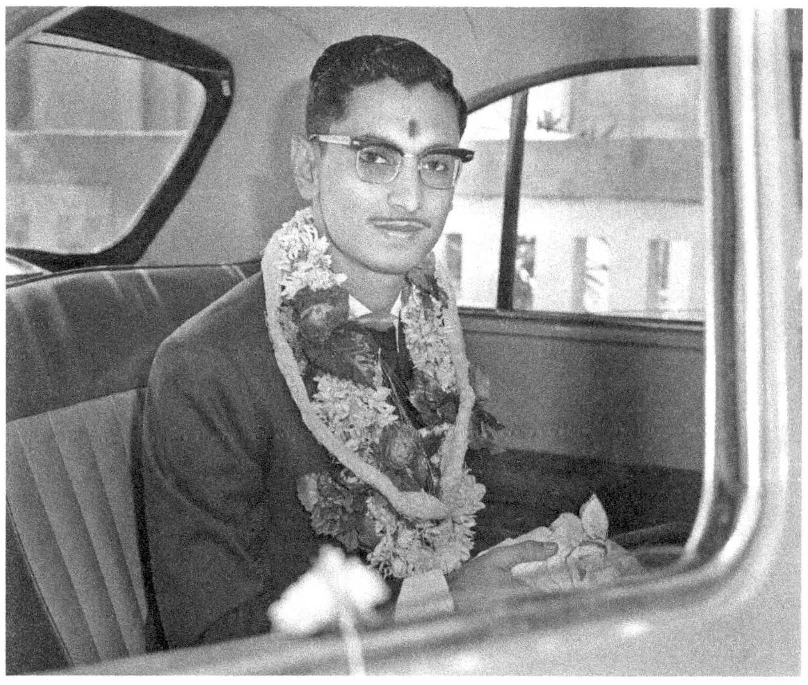

Dad, my friends say you look like a movie star—as if this were a still from a film. You're wearing a garland and something else—it looks like a dried snake—not that I know what a dried snake looks like. Mom tells me it's a kind of garland—khadi from the puja the priest did. You must be 27. I can't do the math. I'll do the math. If it was 1966 and you were born in 1939, then: 1966 – 1939 = 27. Later, I realize I'm wrong. Mom is 21 and you are 26, because it's 1966, but before both of your birthdays. You were born before India's independence, the country still under British rule; I haven't asked you recently what that was like.

The curved windows of the car are the frame. (This photographer is better than the one who shot my wedding.) You are by yourself in the backseat of a car. Your hair is brylcreemed smooth and you are holding a coconut wrapped in cloth (I know it's a coconut from the photos before and after this one); just you and your pencil-thin mustache in an iconic pose—*Shy Groom en Route to His Wedding.* After I study the other photos and talk to Mom, I realize your brothers are already in California and Utah. That's why it's only you in the back of the car.

Why do you look so shy? You aren't now. I had to think about it. You had not seen Mom in seven years, because different continents. You wrote letters and cards from Ahmedabad to Mom in Nairobi. After you married, Mom learned your brother bought the cards for you. You were in medical school and Kirit Kaka was your right-hand man. Your Lakshman, you said, after he passed away.

In this photo you don't yet know you will also move to America. You will start in the Northeast and stay there. Your brothers and parents will urge you to move to California, but you won't. You always do what suits you. You don't know Kirit Kaka will go before you do; none of us know that. He was the first in our family to leave India and the first of your generation to pass. Kirit Kaka is the brother who looks most like you and is just one year younger—but in this picture you look like him.

You're regarding the camera. What are you thinking? Everyone is so excited in the other photographs. (Is that how it was with every wedding? I don't think that's the case.) Your wedding is the first in the family for your parents and Mom's. I see the pride shining on both your mothers' faces—each in a new sari and each wearing a headpiece—also in your father's countenance. (Mom's dad is in East Africa). The joy in these pictures, Dad—the youth! No lines. (If you were in your twenties, Ba was in her forties. I'm older than that now.) All the wedding-goers peering, the procession of men, then the women, one side then the other, the pageantry, the ritual joining of families. One young boy, it looks like Jayesh, in shorts and barefoot, walking in front of Dada and the other men. You, too, must have once been the youngest boy at someone else's wedding.

It's hard for me to see this photo outside of its place in the album. The photos are glued to thick black construction paper: Each page has one picture only. They do give the appearance of film stills, each with its own story. A beautiful but irritating album—it won't lie flat, which is why I've never studied these photos before. I realize now I've never seen you and Mom look at this album either. I wish this were a triptych instead of a single image. I want to remember you in motion.

The look on your face, it's one I see on your grandson who is most like me. I see here how he resembles you. You've got those Malcolm X glasses (both your grandsons have them now, too; everything comes back). You are not yet who you will be. I mean, you are already a surgeon, but you are not yet American, not yet a father, not yet a husband who will retrain in medicine in order to stay in another country, not a grandfather with acute myeloid leukemia, not someone undergoing chemo, not an octogenarian.

Look at those starched cuffs—the angles: With your brothers in the States, who starched and ironed them? They told me they did the ironing. (It irritated you that I never offered to iron your shirts. But I never iron anything). In the photos before and after this one I can see your cufflinks—I forgot you ever wore them; that I would open the dresser drawer in the blue room and study them and finger the shapes as I did with Mom's pendant and hoop and clip-on earrings, her bangles and necklaces, her filmy scarves, to see how they worked. These same cufflinks became relics living in a drawer alongside your handkerchiefs—but you still use handkerchiefs. Your hands have a tremor. Forget cufflinks, forget ironing: You no longer wear suits or ties.

Now you sit in a chair that helps you get up, the one we bought for InduBa. You didn't think we should buy one back then. You didn't think you would need one. It's an adjustable height armchair with a remote control, a Power Lift Recliner—the most American name.

You walk with a walker now. Time is a snake, paused then moving; or a river, still then snaking; or a garland winding its way, serpentine—a length of homespun cotton; an ellipse of fragrant flowers in bloom, then drying. *You think it's not going to happen to you*, you say. *We were young. Then one day you wake up and you're old.*

It's a warning. And reminder. *But Dad*, it's still hard to mind it.

---

*I had been working on this essay for about a month and read a draft to my father over lunch. The essay was going to be published in a book, I told him. *People are actually interested in this kind of thing?* He shook his head and returned to eating his DiBella's sub. I finished the essay a few weeks after that and was corresponding with Dinah on edits when my dad passed. I'm grateful to have had "Serpentine" to offer as a reading at the gathering for my father on June 13, 2023.

CLIFFORD THOMPSON
ON THE STREET WITH THE THREE RED BRICK HOUSES

"He wants to take a picture of us," my maternal grandmother, Maggie, said to my great uncle Manson. We stood behind the three red brick houses where my immediate and extended families lived, in those yards with their indistinct borders. This was the spring of 1986; I was twenty-three, Manson around eighty-seven, Maggie ninety-two. I had a new camera and was enamored of black and white film, which I thought gave subjects an old, classic look, and the way my grandmother and uncle arranged themselves for me harked back to that early way of being in photographs, to the attitude of generations now gone: no smiling, certainly no mugging. This was serious.

Once upon a time, in rural Virginia, Maggie was married to Manson's older brother Robert, my grandfather. Fifteen years before I was born, Robert died, after which Maggie joined many of my relatives on both sides of my family in Washington, DC. She moved in with my parents, eventually going to live with them on the street with the three red brick houses, where I grew up. When I was very young, I shared a bedroom with my older sisters and my grandmother, and my grandmother and I shared a bed. By the time of my earliest memories, she could barely hear. She rarely left the house; one day when I was about nine, she asked me to take a walk with her up the street, which I remember so clearly because that was the single time it happened. When I came home for lunch in elementary school, Maggie fixed my meals. She watched soaps, whose plots she guessed from the characters' actions; she ate her last meal of the day, which she called her dinner, at noon, using hardened gums from which teeth had long ago disappeared; she talked sparingly, and also loudly, because she couldn't hear herself. Sometimes I overheard her prayers. One phrase stands out in my memory: "Don't let me go blind."

In that way of children, I thought—because I didn't think—that my grandmother had always been as she was. The same with Uncle Manson, who lived two houses away with his wife, Lucy, dead four years when I took this photo. (The house in between belonged to my father's older sister and her husband, my mother's first cousin.) Maggie and Manson's job in life was to be old people. Now, as I make impressive progress toward being an old person myself, I wonder: Did Maggie ever look at

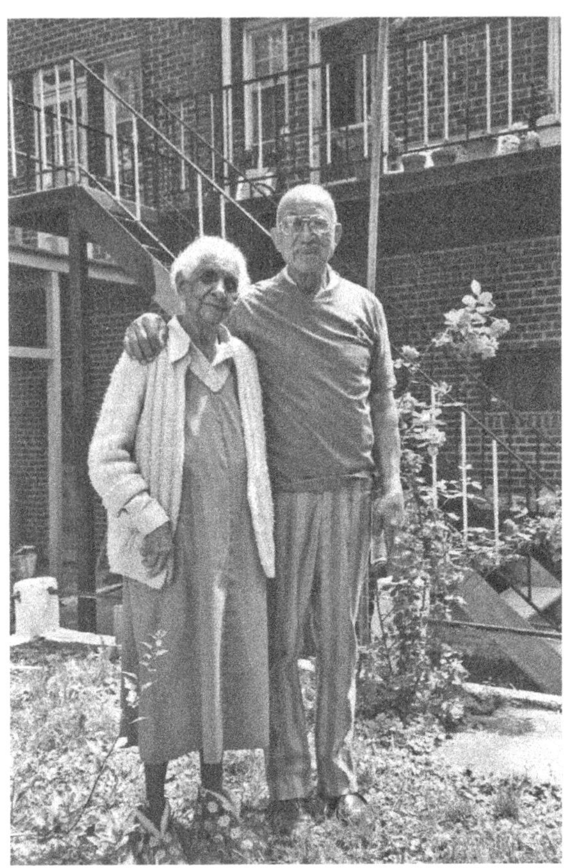

Manson and see her husband? Did Manson ever ponder his brother's choice of a wife? Nothing they said or did during my childhood suggested any of this. Like all adults who visited our house—and most of those were relatives—Uncle Manson would shout when he talked to my grandmother, not about anything important, and not seeming to wonder if he'd been heard, which he hadn't; my grandmother would talk back. Two loud winds blowing in opposite directions:

"How you doing?"

"How's Lucy?"

"She's doing fine—"

"Fine!

This was serious. That is to say: The expressions in the photograph are earned. The autumn that I was nineteen and home on a break from college, I sat with Uncle Manson in his living room, which had the same small dimensions and intricate molding as ours but was decorated differently, like the same model wearing another outfit. I mentioned the work I had done that summer, delivering packages on foot for an office supply store. "I don't mean to dispute you," he said, "but you don't know what work is." Sitting next to me another time, years later, Manson gave me to understand that I didn't know how things had once been; neither, he said, mentioning their names, did most others in our family. But, he told me, Maggie knew. Here in the city, Manson had worked in industrial kitchens until his retirement, which left him, in my mother's words, with "nothing to do and a lot of time to do it in." But back in the rural, segregated Virginia of the early twentieth century, as Manson gave me to understand, his work, and Maggie's, had been survival. He remembered, and he knew that she did, too. That conversation, it seems to me now, was all I ever heard about Maggie and Manson's thoughts and feelings toward each other.

But apparently that is not all there was. Sometime in the early 1990s, Manson was hospitalized. After a time he recovered and was driven home. The odd thing about what happened next is that I can picture it vividly, though I was only told about it, and though it is so utterly different from anything I ever observed about one of the people involved. From the open door of our house, Maggie, in her upper nineties by then, saw Manson get out of the car; my grandmother, whom I rarely saw walk anywhere, burst from the house, arms thrown wide, shouting as she ran toward my uncle, "I didn't think I'd see you no more!"

SUZANNE BERNE
THE CELEBRATION

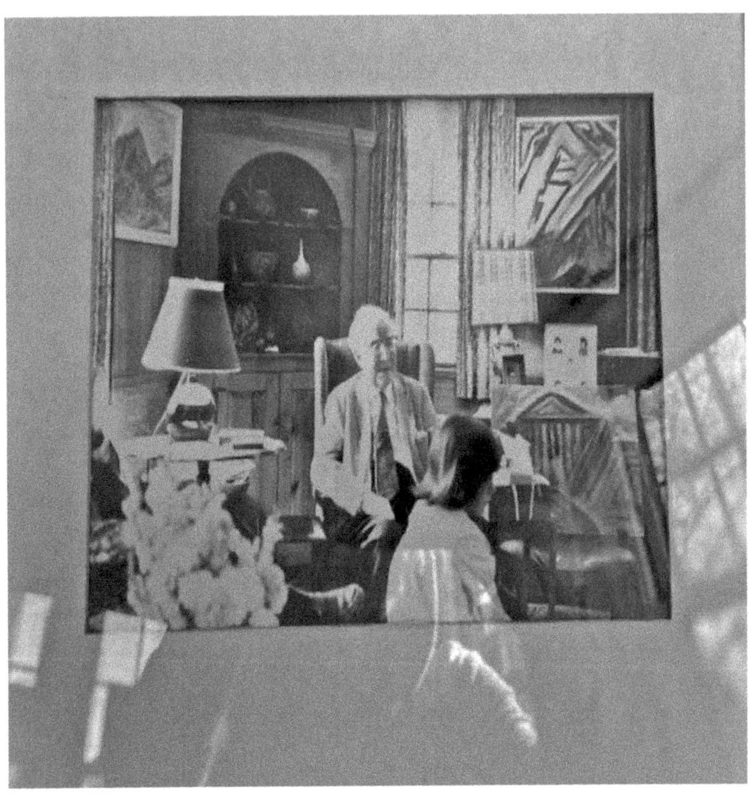

It looks more like a private exhibition than a party. In the center is my grandfather, wearing a camel's hair coat and a tie, seated in a wingchair and illuminated by two lamps and a bright window. On display are three of his oil paintings, all featuring mountains in vivid, geometrical strokes. His most recent canvas, a Grecian temple emerging from mountains, is propped on an ottoman. A dark recessed wooden hutch behind him holds another display, of modern pottery. Also displayed are photographs of grandchildren, including my older brother Henry, the photographer. It is August 9, 1970, my grandfather's 93rd birthday, on Cape Cod. He eats dinner at exactly six o'clock every night, always in a coat and tie, even when alone (a widower for 40 years), even on the hottest days of summer. So, it must be around five o'clock, cocktail hour, which is why the windows brim with daylight, though because it is technically evening the lamps are on.

In the foreground of that crowded room sits my younger sister in a dress with puffed sleeves, looking away from our grandfather although he's clearly speaking. He must be telling a story we've all heard before, probably about leaving Cincinnati at the turn of the century to study music in Berlin: climbing the Matterhorn in his one pair of shoes with a bar of chocolate in his pocket, visiting Napoleon's tomb and "standing beside history," studying piano with the same teacher as Artur Rubenstein, then a boy in short pants. Also pictured, half hidden by a flash of flowers, is my father's foot, in a brown leather loafer. Though the foot appears motionless, it was joggling up and down. I know this because my father often joggles his foot when he crosses one leg over the other and because as soon my grandfather begins talking, on any subject, my father starts fidgeting. The flowers are a present from my mother, who loves my grandfather and regrets his loneliness, and is always pained by his son's impatient foot.

My brother's intention in this sepia-colored photograph was, presumably, to capture a patriarch being celebrated by his family on his birthday. What he's caught is restlessness and clashing, best conveyed by that plaid lampshade fighting with the curtains. My grandfather is a born Victorian, with his decorous coat and tie at dinner, his reverence for pre-war Europe, his punctilious observance of time—he's also a burning modernist, as is clear from those abstract expressionist oils, which he's so anxious to have admired. Every morning he works for three or four hours in a bare little studio beside his garage, producing hundreds of vibrant, turbulent canvases. So much energy and effort from this small, formal, fragile old man. So much mountain climbing with his fierce paintbrush.

Met with … my father's foot, my sister's averted glance, my mother's apologetic bouquet. Outside that shut window is a dazzling August late afternoon and a breeze full of salt. Quail run across the grass, gulls cry over the bay, the sky vaults into a pure dizzying blue. Inside, shadows are massing. The hutch yawns like a cave full of shards. That Grecian temple is a tomb.

*

What's on exhibit here, I suppose, is how one person's passions can bore everyone else to death, and that birthday parties for the very old will be sepia-tinted, and too obviously dutiful. Yet what I see in this over-exposed photograph is radiance. Those flowers are incandescent and so is that old man, alight with his own sensibility, which he refuses to find quaint, judging by those jagged landscapes full of arpeggios and treble clefs. He's not from the past, he's suffused with pastness. Devouring his chocolate bar atop the Matterhorn in everyday shoes, standing self-consciously beside Napoleon, sitting on a hard chair in a Berlin hallway, listening with jealous awe to a boy genius practicing his scales. So what if he never played the piano like Artur Rubenstein? So what if no one thinks much of his paintings and his grandchildren would rather be eating hotdogs on the beach than marking time in puffed sleeves before his birthday cake? He has stood beside history, was *there* during the huge turnings of the past century. A man who came of age before the world was lit by lightbulbs and rang with telephones. Before Novocain. Before jazz. Before highways and contrails and split atoms. A man who heard different rests and silences than we can hear now, who saw more stars.

Every year, I worry that this is my grandfather's last birthday. How much older can he get? My mother insists he's very healthy, "well preserved," she says, and it's true that when I lean in to kiss his soft cheek, he smells of beer and turpentine, a strangely fresh and stirring smell.

3 MIRROR, MIRROR

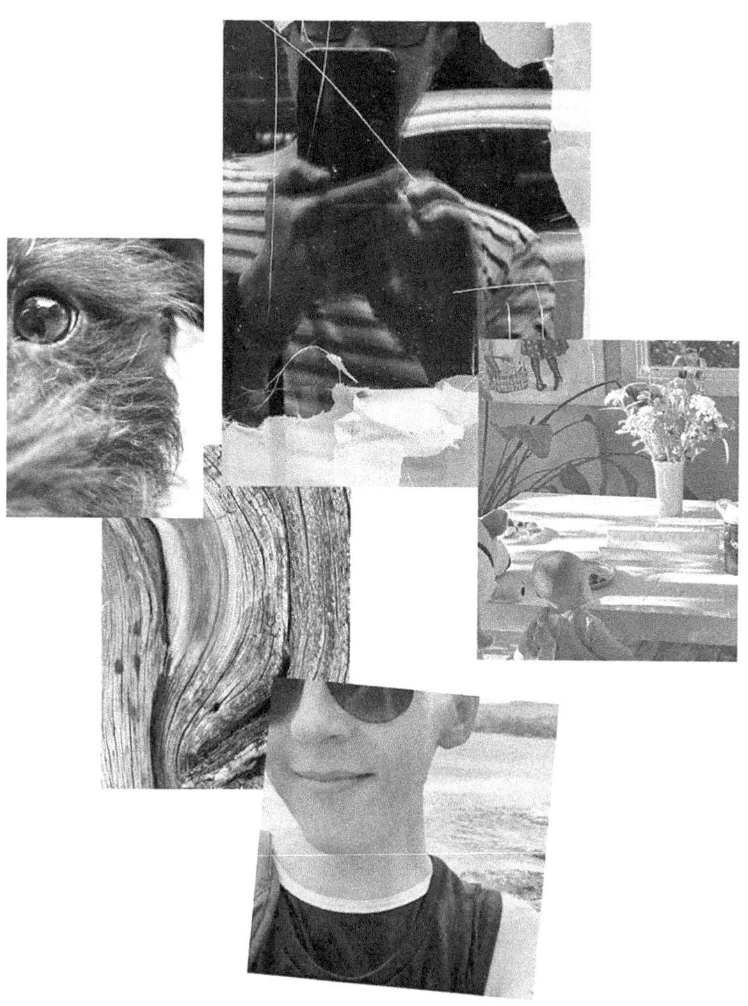

"First, the selfie, the first you had ever taken in which you looked like this."

ALEX MARZANO-LESNEVICH

HANNAH HOWARD
THIS IS THE START OF A WEDNESDAY

I don't have an alarm clock these days.

I have "mommy, mommy, mommy, mommy." I have kid tears that come from deep in the belly and shrieks of laughter that rise up from the toes, half-heard from bed.

It's 6 or 7 AM. My head is still fuzzy. Once up, the first thing I do is hit "brew now" on the coffeemaker. Then I pour two milks. They have to be identical. They have to be full, to the top. They have to be at the edge of the kitchen counter, so little arms can reach them.

Next I pee. I take my birth control pill and my Zoloft, which I'm tapering down, so only half a pill now, which I break with my fingernail. It's sort of crumbly.

I always try to smile when I open the door to their room. It's a sliding door, and it makes a sort of whooshing sound. In this room they share there's a big girl bed, with a headboard full of stickers and sticker residue, and a blue crib. When I see their faces for the first time today (since some middle-of-the-night emergency involving a missing sock), they look different. They look older. Fundamentally changed. My daughter's hair is stuck to one side of her head. My son's pajama shirt has lifted up so the roundness of his belly pokes out. I want to kiss it. He stands up, his hands wrapped around the sides of the crib. His full body grin makes me want to cry. I've always been a crier. In all our wedding pictures, my eyes are shiny with tears.

The light is still soupy and I haven't had coffee before I have little hands on my face, my arms, around my thighs. Soft skin and squirmy legs. Tears and snot and mysterious tackiness (we had a bath last night—why?). Chaos.

One hour later I take this picture; this is my mom and my daughter; this is the light in the kitchen in the morning. By this time, we have had our milks and our coffee (two cups). We have read *Cloudy with a Chance of Meatballs*. We have watched *Peppa Pig*. I have done the Wordle, and

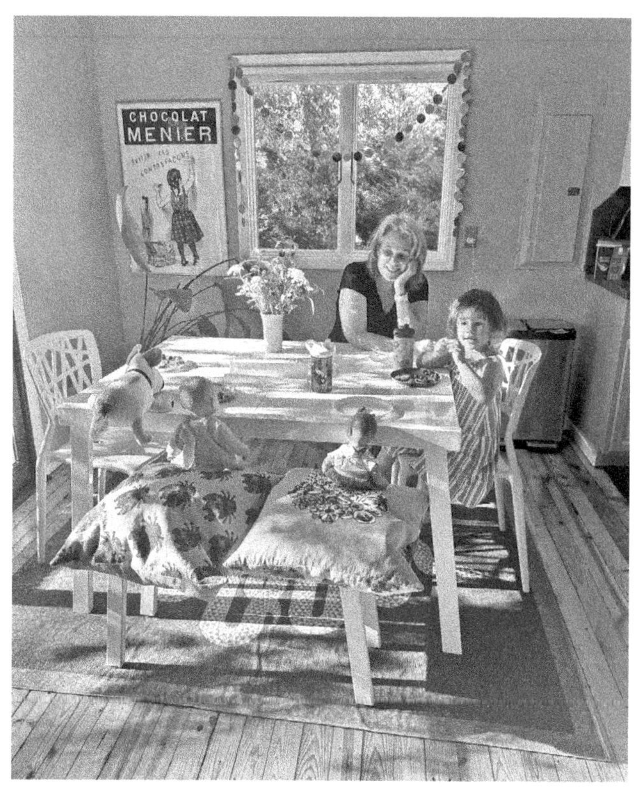

changed a poopy diaper, and dressed two wiggly wormy small people. We have read *Cloudy with a Chance of Meatballs* again.

My mom has come over to help us get ready for preschool summer camp. I've never seen so much of her, not since I was a kid. She and my daughter have set the breakfast table for her dolls, her dog, herself, and her baby brother who is not a baby anymore. (Meanwhile, he's spinning in circles, collapsing on the floor with giddiness and dizziness. He doesn't want breakfast. He wants what he wants.)

What she wants:

For the dolls to have real berries, not pretend food.
Blueberries, not raspberries.
The purple plate. No not THAT purple plate.

To wear a party dress to preschool.
Not THAT party dress.
To wear her shoes on the wrong feet.
To sit on my lap and for her brother, wherever he is, to MOVE.

But soon they will be at school, and the house will be quiet. I'll put the pillows back on the couch and move my laptop to the kitchen table. Our (real) dog will curl up near my feet, in a patch of sunshine. I will write.

When I became a mom, my tears became a little more desperate. (The Zoloft has helped, but not enough to change my fundamental self.) I'm saying, when I pick them up at 3, they will be fundamentally changed all over again. I will want to cry, but I will hold it together—probably.

ALEX MARZANO-LESNEVICH
THE DISTANCE

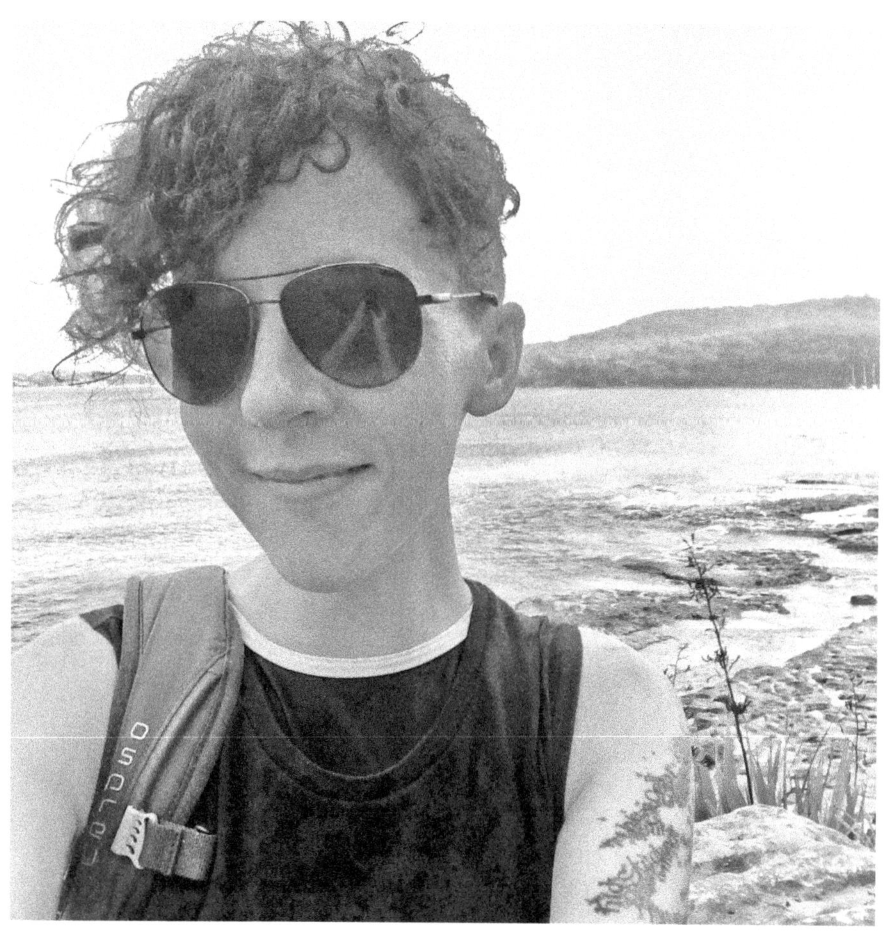

After you stepped over a threshold on the other side of the world, triggering the ding of the barber's unseen bell. After you watched her rope your long hair into a braid and you didn't cry; loop her fingers through scissors and you didn't cry; sever that braid and you didn't cry, and you weren't yet taking testosterone so that wasn't the reason you didn't cry. This was a moment to be rushed through, because beyond it lay your whole life. You only had to do it. If you also had to feel, well, twenty years had already passed that way.

After you felt air on the back of your head for the first time. After you stared in the mirror and the person who stared back was both you and not you, vulnerable as a plucked chicken. You had posed for one last photograph before the scissors, but already you knew you'd never be able to look at it. What was a trophy shot of? Discomfort you'd mistaken for your skin. Despair that had been animal in your chest.

After the bell rang a second time, and you could no longer hear it, the years gone making a kind of white noise in your head. After you walked three blocks in that fugue, spotted a men's clothing store, and hooked left. After you stood fingering the fabrics, as though the scissors had snipped your voice from your throat, and the two sales guys watched you. After you imagined what they were thinking, tried to puzzle out who they thought you were, and then you imagined the shape of your body through their eyes—who that shape perhaps made them think you were—and you kicked that idea right out of your brain like a drunk out of a bar. After you thought, for the first of what would be a thousand times, a million, a lifetime, *no*. After you understood that you would have to guard not just yourself against others, but yourself against yourself this way.

After you asked, finally, to try on a pair of pants. And a jacket. And a shirt. And you pulled the clothes over your body, holding your breath at your hips your chest *keep going keep going don't feel keep going* and raised your gaze to the mirror and saw, for the first time, that body, your body, with short hair and a suit. Still you didn't cry. But you did say that you would like to try on everything in the store, please, yes you did mean everything.

You had decided you would go to the beach afterwards, so you did. Again clothing, so again *don't think don't feel*. After you yanked a tight top over your chest and quickly a black muscle t over that and only then paused and noticed the way your short hair now made a kind of echo off the flat chest and thought, *okay, this maybe*. You rode the tram to the park and walked to the beach and saw the gorgeous verdant green, observed it like fact, *beauty*, like a thing you stood back from.

After you noticed that you noticed the distance between you and the world. That you didn't just live the distance, but could see it. That was new. And you stood in the water and it was *cool* and the sky was a gorgeous *blue* and there were children playing at the water's edge and you thought, *laughter*. And *this must be what grief feels like*, though you couldn't yet say what you were grieving. Time, maybe. Mortality, maybe. That this had taken you your whole life so far. That if you could feel, you were probably going to have to hurt.

Before you used the language for who you were. Before your smile loosened and your shoulders dropped. Before having a body, and watching yourself have a body, turned into, sometimes, being a body. Before your skin coarsened and your wrinkles deepened and zits became your constant companion. Before age and the hormone needles' injections worked their separate transformations. Before you thought about surgeries, decided no, decided yes, decided no again. Before you and your face struck up a kind of peace. Before you, so much later in life than you'd have imagined possible, made peace with the idea of peace.

Afterward came the journey home. Three planes, two continents, one ocean, countless rivers and tributaries and lives passed below, bodies and minds and hearts with sleeping wishes and hidden insides and so many worlds held secret within this one, for which you dressed in the clothes you had bought in the shop, still unwilling to take them off, twenty-six hours in a stiff blazer and button-down shirt. Afterward came the "sir" from one security officer and the "ma'am" from another, the "sir-I'm-sorry-ma'am" from one kiosk clerk and the "ma'am-I'm-sorry-sir" from another. Afterward, the knowledge that gender was like borders, slippery and permeable and only sometimes marked, invented and policed with violence, a collective fever dream. Afterward, theory became a thing you lived with your body.

But at the ocean there was an ice cream cone and a selfie. First, the selfie, the first you had ever taken in which you looked like this. Later the hair would get shorter, later testosterone would broaden your jaw, but first there was this first.

Then waxy unfamiliar bills you pressed into a vendor's hand, the choice of vanilla because it was the choice of your childhood, the pleasing scratch of the cone's texture against your palm. You wandered away from the cart in a daze, your gaze on the turquoise horizon, understanding now that distance was what had made this possible. Made you possible. You stood under a tree and your tongue met the cold dairy and you felt it melt and slip and give way, yielding into sweetness like all the years you had just shed.

You kept rubbing the back of your head then. You palmed the soft bristles of your scalp like a new lover. You didn't know what was coming, you couldn't, but you stood companion now to all your fears and all your hopes, the weight of what was to come suddenly as vast and deep and frightening and beautiful as the blue expanse before you, and your grief was so huge you trembled with it. All you had for so long feared. All you had, you realized, just chosen.

But as your tongue met the ice cream again, and your life before slipped into your life after, you looked up and were surprised to meet the eyes of a woman. Who was, you realized, watching you lick the cone. No—watching your tongue. No—staring. And who, when she noticed you noticing, suddenly blushed a deep pink. The pink of a sunset, the pink of a sunrise, the pink of both ending and beginning.

And, so in the middle of goddamn weighty everything, you also thought: *Oh. This is going to be fun.*

ATTICA LOCKE
MACINTOSH

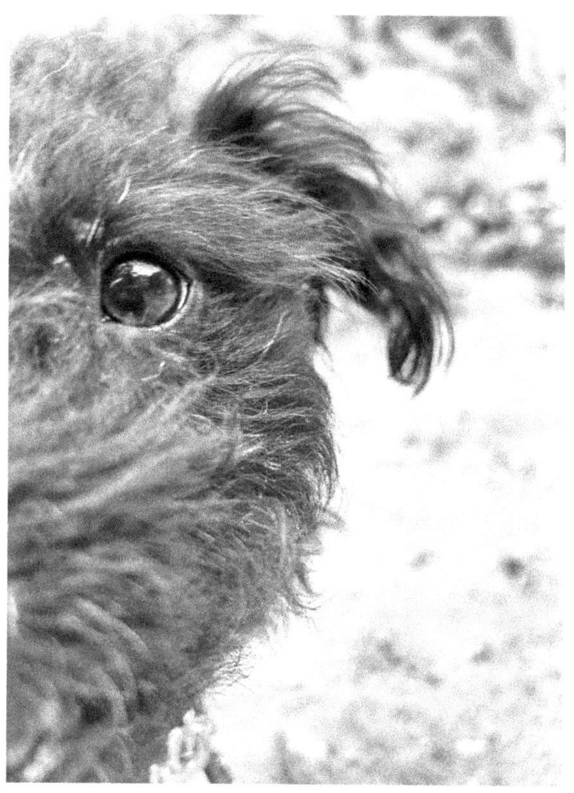

I don't like dogs.

I am four years old visiting my aunt and uncle in Baton Rouge.
They have Dobermans.
So big, we ride them as horses, my cousin and me.
They are outdoor dogs, as I remember most dogs in the late 70s
were.
(Could that be right? Did everyone used to keep their dogs outside?)
I am in my pajamas. We are watching *Dallas*. Or maybe that's a trick
of memory.

Maybe it's a Saturday, and we're watching the *Love Boat* or *Fantasy Island* (if they let us stay up that late enough for Ricardo Montalbán and that weird, creepy show).
It doesn't matter. The show isn't the point.
The point is that the dogs get into the house, and race through the living room's shag carpet, running over me and my cousin, where we lie on the floor watching TV.
The button to this story that I used to tell people when they asked if I like dogs:
All I remember is dog genitalia in my face.

I don't like dogs.
Apparently, we had two twin dachshunds at one point.
Coffee and Donut.
I don't remember this so much as I remember being told this as a fact of my life.
Although, rarely does anyone mention Coffee and Donut anymore.
Sometimes I wonder if I made up the whole thing.
They were hit by a car.
Both?
At the same time?
This seems apocryphal.

I don't like dogs.
I do remember Pepper though.
He? She?
I don't remember their gender.
I don't remember getting the dog.
She stayed at my dad's house after the divorce.
I would have been seven or eight.
I don't remember walking Pepper.
I don't remember playing with Pepper.
I only remember trying to get my father's attention when he was on a call one day.
Pepper looks funny.
He's not breathing right.
Daddy was on a call. He was a lawyer with a small practice.
Every call, every client mattered.
Pepper had died by the time he got off the phone.

It is the only real memory I have of Pepper.
I remember the trauma.

Speaking of trauma, what about all the dogs they trained to hunt enslaved people?
Isn't that shit in my DNA?
Big dogs *do* scare me.
Do I not like dogs on an epigenetic level?

I had a cat once.
I remember liking the cat.
But she ran away.
Sauntered is more like it. Cha-cha-cha-ed down the street.
She moved to another kid's house in my neighborhood in middle school.
On the bus, the kid told me, I have your cat.
I don't remember the cat's name, only her disloyalty.
My reaction to the kid of the bus was basically, *keep her then.*

I don't like pets.
I don't want animals in my house.

I told all of this to my daughter from the first time she asked for a dog, at eight.
Then again when she was ten.
And again when she was twelve.
We're not getting a dog.

We make plans and God laughs, the saying goes.
Well, from 2016 to 2021, God was doing quite a set at the Laugh Factory that is the Universe, with a few particularly cruel jokes at the expense of the Western Hemisphere.
From Trump to the pandemic to several failed impeachments to an insurrection to the fact it snows in Texas these days, and Europe is frequently in triple digits.

I happen to have a bright, deeply feeling child for whom the world is chaos. I looked at my husband one day and said, *Let's get a dog.*
He said he'd been thinking the same thing.
I was only doing this for her, of course.

Thanksgiving, 2021. As a family, we closed out the night by perusing shelter and rescue agency websites on our individual devices, holding up photos of dogs to share when one of us felt a connection, then sighing heavily when the other ones found some reason that dog wasn't the one. This went on for hours. And then someone, and I don't remember who, said, *MacIntosh* and held up their phone. We all looked at him, and some energy moved between the three of us. We stopped cold. My husband, my daughter, and I all said, *Yes.*

We met him the next day. In an upstairs storeroom over a pet store, he licked my daughter's face and melted into her arms. He sat in my husband's lap. And he was curious about me . . . this woman who has always believed, *I don't like dogs.*

He was small and warm and wiggly in my arms. He licked *my* face, and I *did* flinch.

But I also felt something radiating from his little body. *Love.*

His entire essence is curiosity and love. I knew that somehow fate had brought this little being into our lives.

MacIntosh is now my little sweetie, my little booger bear, my boogie, my scruffaluffagus, my little skunklebutt. He is one of my great loves. And I have turned into a crazy person about him. The first time I took him to the vet for a procedure for which he wasn't allowed to eat ahead of time, I refused to eat in front of him. I hand feed him sometimes. We take naps together. I marvel at the pureness of his heart and presence in the world. I know everyone says this about their dogs, but he is absolutely perfect. (Maybe we're *all* right.)

I still like to say, *I'm not a dog person. I'm a MacIntosh person.*

But the truth is, MacIntosh's love has changed how I see the world.

It's not that I like dogs now so much as I understand them better.

I've long known that every human has a story.

I know I'm late at forty-nine to realize that so too does every dog; each their own story, each their own soul.

I am a wiser woman because of that sweet little face.

I have more patience and hope about the wildly uncertain times in which we are living.

And I am forever grateful to the Great Comedienne in the Sky for bringing him to me.

WAYNE KOESTENBAUM

TORN SELF-PORTRAIT WITH STRIPED SHIRT

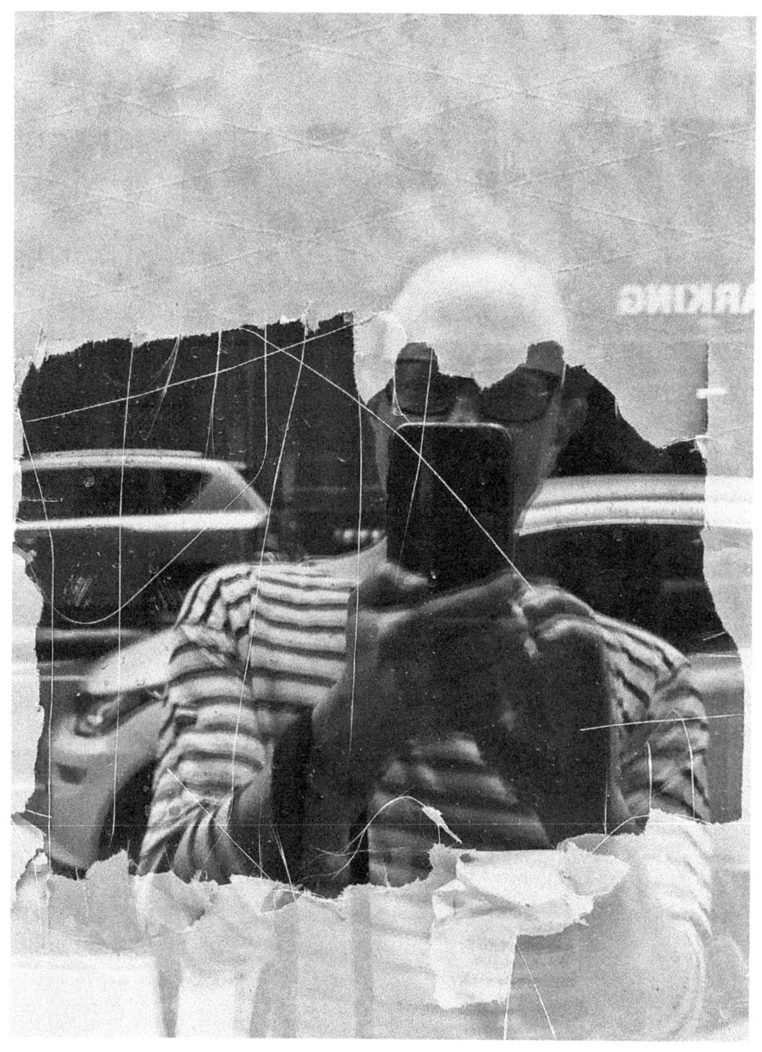

I took a walk and found my reflection in a torn spot. Where precisely? On a damaged rectangle of paper draped over a store window. The store was closed, under repair, seeking remedy. Part of the paper, covering the window, was ripped. The paper's job was to conceal and protect the window. The paper made a mess of its task. The paper failed to meet its obligations. Inside that failed area I found the mirrored image of myself, a photographer, wearing a marinière, a boat-neck striped shirt. I wasn't in Saint-Malo or Quimper. I was in midtown Manhattan, in 2021, during the pandemic. The most characteristic trait in the photo is my right shoulder, its tension, its avoidance of repose. (Do I detect a ghost of a bicep in my right arm?) My raised shoulder offers ballast for the hand that grasps an iPhone, a recording device that conceals my jaw, mouth, cheeks, and most of my nose. My right hand clutches the phone with a tight grip that recalls my mother's hand, long ago, clenching a red Papermate ballpoint pen. It might have been blue. I've already written about that Papermate, and my mother's hand, holding it. She kept her pens in a cup beside the downstairs phone. Long ago, her phone number, mine also, was 408-252-3801. That numerical sequence was my identity for nearly eighteen years. The 252 bespeaks symmetry and godliness. We were a godly household and a symmetrical household. The 3801 suggests a welcome variousness. We were a various household, given to sweetmeats. What were our sweetmeats? Tension was one of our sweetmeats. Hiding our faces was one of our sweetmeats. Avoiding the topic was one of our sweetmeats. Repetition was one of our sweetmeats. I keep accidentally typing "sweatmeat" instead of "sweetmeat." Notice, I'm inserting sweat in the place of sweetness. We were not a sweaty household though our phone number was 408-252-3801. We didn't like sports. We took showers infrequently. Once a week was the protocol for showers. My penis would begin to stink, in the days when my phone number was 408-252-3801. I could peel a curl of smegma from around the rim of my glans. I'd take a washcloth, wet and soapy, to my organ, in the bathroom that was known as the "kid's bathroom," to distinguish it from my parent's bathroom, which was the master's. My mother was the master. She was a woman of no sweat and much tension. Her repose did not take place in my father's arms. Perhaps he offered repose more frequently than I realized. The 8 in our phone number was an infinity sweetmeat. We would go on forever, I was confident of that fact. Our immortality was sewn into the heart of our tension. My right shoulder in the self-portrait is the sweetmeat memento, the proof of tension and of failed repose, failed because I didn't seek it. Photography is repose, and so now I seek photography, black-and-white especially, because it steals colors away from me. I don't deserve colors. And I don't deserve a full self-portrait, just torn pieces, discarded sigils, garbage-like crullers, crabbed and nonce. I've discovered a new website. It's called Sniffies. You can instantly find men. I cruise Sniffies but don't hook up. I am a Sniffies bystander. From Sniffies I've learned a helpful phrase: pump-and-dump. In the days when my phone number was 408-252-3801, I didn't know about pump-and-dump, though the "1" in my phone number sings the song of pump-and-dump, a sweetmeat aria for one voice without accompaniment. Logic decrees that when you post a selfie on a website like Sniffies, you will choose the most flattering photo, but an attractive image is not necessarily accurate. So it's better to post an unflattering selfie. But if you put forward a less attractive snapshot, no one will seek you out. Torn between the Scylla and Charybdis of flattering and unflattering depictions, I remain a detached chronicler of the online bacchanal. My favorite activity these days is using a hole-puncher to punch out small holes from 16mm films I've purchased on eBay. I bought an educational film from the 1960s, *What Do Flowers Do.* Using my hole-puncher, I punched out tiny circles from *What Do Flowers Do,* and then, with clear Scotch tape, affixed these circles of informative emulsion onto clear leader. Leader is the blank footage at the beginnings and ends of films. You can't thread precious footage into the projector. You need to creep into its gate with crummy, dispensable leader. Leader is a delicate way of beginning your conversation with the optical machine, which wants to eat up your film. I bought 200 feet of clear leader from a film supply shop in Illinois, along with a 16mm clip from an unspecified 1970s movie. A woman—I don't know the actor's name—enters a bedroom where Richard Harris is waiting. Or maybe Harris walks into the room where this unidentified woman is waiting. I put the two-minute clip in a bucket with a few capfuls of Clorox and swirled the solution around for a few minutes, to bleach out most of the information from the film. On the newly blank portions of this Richard Harris bedroom clip, I taped tiny circles of *What Do Flowers Do.* My finished hybrid-film, a collage, alternates between botany and bedrooms. What you need to remember from this essay is the word *sweetmeat* as a substitute for unattainable satisfaction. You say *sweetmeat* when you are ravenous but are not at liberty to discuss your appetite.

PICO IYER
MY SHADOW SELF

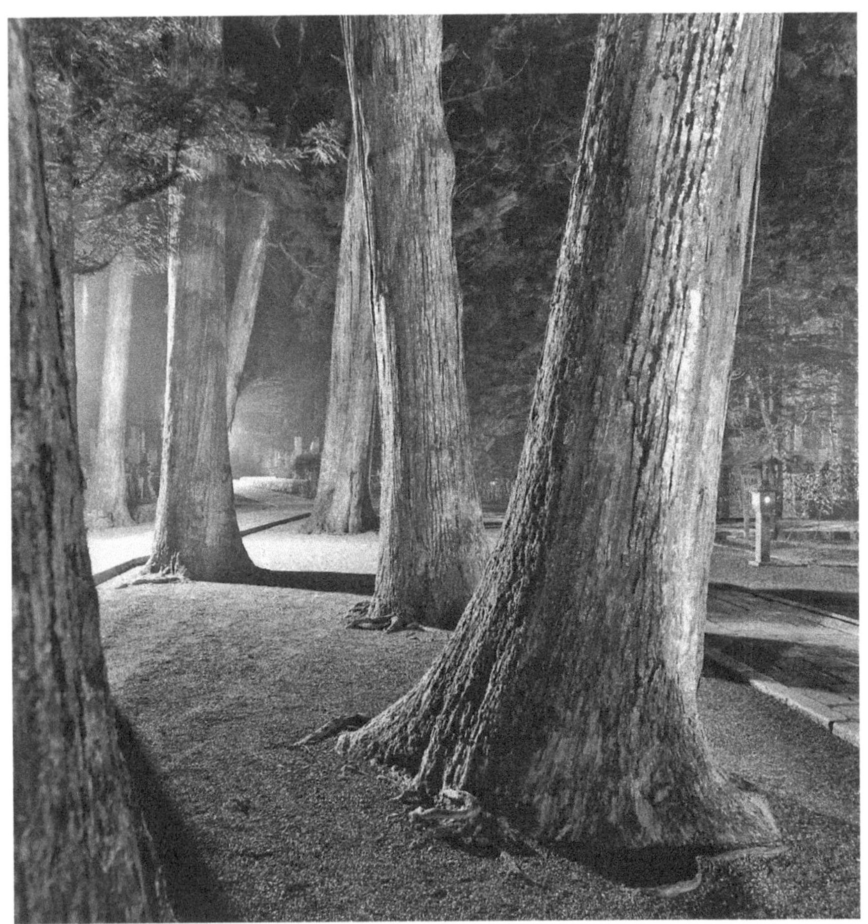

Photo credit: Michael Kenna

A pandemic had brought the entire world to a standstill. My mother, eighty-eight, had been rushed into a hospital in an ambulance, losing blood. I took three flights through eerily deserted airports to be with her after she emerged, and then we waited, for an end that never seemed to come.

We're always, all of us, living in a state of uncertainty, but lockdown brought that home with shivering intensity. Death was breathing, loudly, in the next room. We had no sense of when—or whether—the cloud would ever lift. Every day, at the dinner table, my mother looked through me as if I were the ghost. I started writing about paradise, since the only contentment I could trust would be one found in the midst of life—and in the face of death.

Our social lives were radically overturned. Proust, Melville, Emily Dickinson became my daily companions; friends I hadn't heard from in years wrote to say hello.

One morning I received a message from a celebrated photographer: Might I contribute words to a book on the Buddha he was putting together? I wrote back to say yes, and soon we were exchanging long and zesty messages almost every day even as the project was put on hold.

Michael had studied photography just outside Oxford, we found, at the same time I was studying literature not many miles away. He and I had moved to the American West Coast in exactly the same year; we'd alighted on Japan—our secret second home—in the very same season, a decade later.

Michael had spent six years training to be a Catholic priest; I now spent much of my time in a Benedictine hermitage. Twice, I now recalled, I'd written articles on cherished places near my apartment in Japan, and both times a wise editor had invited Michael to supply the photographs.

When my book on hope in the midst of darkness was complete, I reported this to my new friend, and he, on a whim, sent me fifteen images of a mystical mountain in the heart of Japan. I hadn't told him that my book all but concluded in that site.

I thought to share them with my editor and instantly she realized that one of them—the one that had possessed me, too—would be the perfect cover for my book: a black-and-white image of a graveyard at the dead of night, taken with an hour-long exposure that brought eerie light and spectral shadows into the dark.

"That's you!" cried my wife, as soon as I showed it to her. "The perfect picture of who you are, deep down."

They say every portrait is, under cover, a self-portrait. But in the case of Michael Kenna's cover-photo for my book, it seemed, more hauntingly, a picture of the self that neither of us had met. Of him and me and everything we shared. Right at the heart of that forest of graves, a light burning through the night.

4 WISH YOU WERE HERE

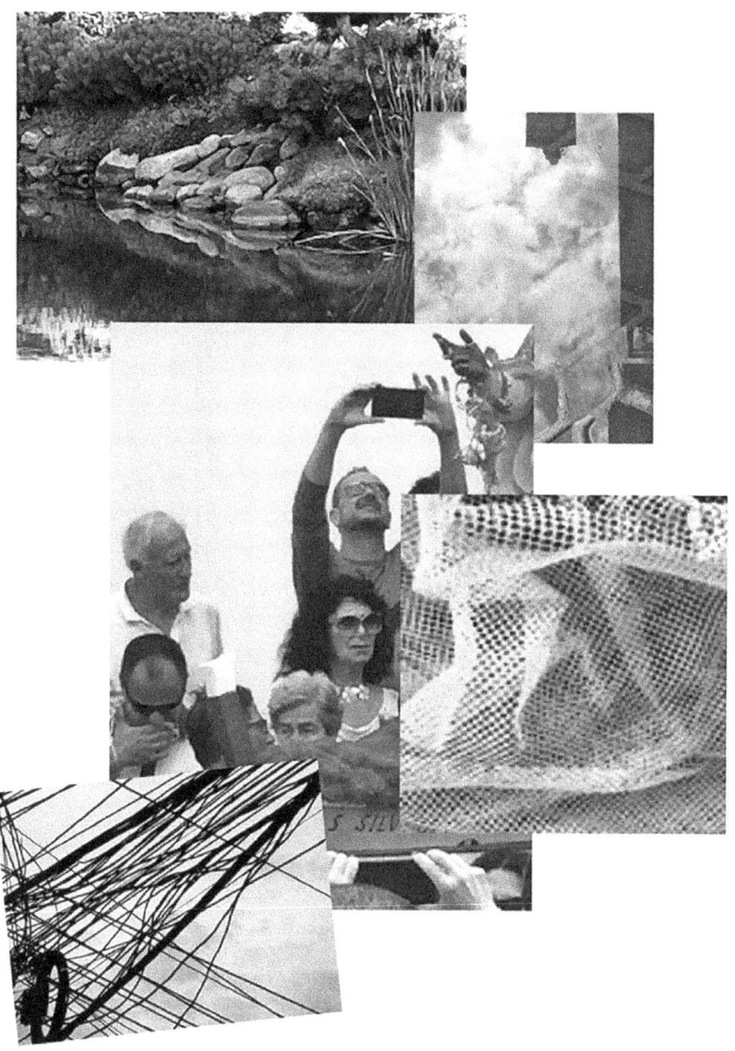

"So much of
my being belongs
to this place."

LYNELL GEORGE

IVY POCHODA
GARDEN

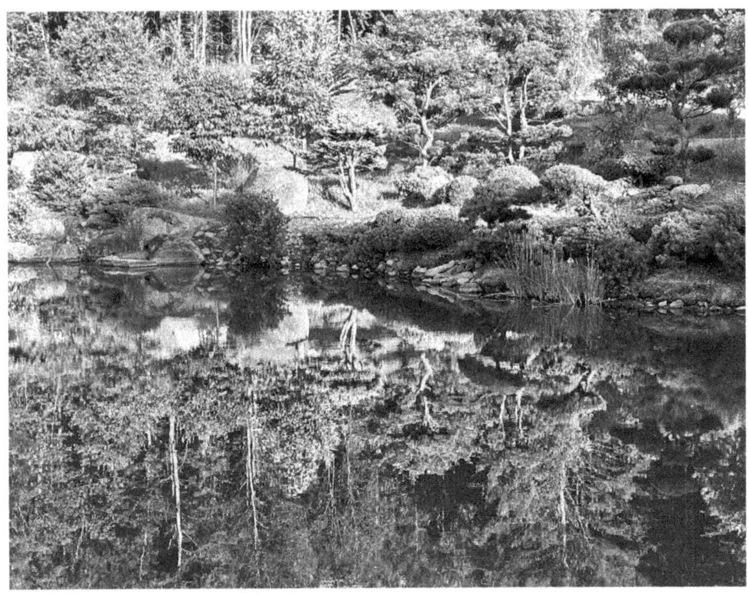

My father took up cooking after my parents separated in 1990. He was not known for being detail oriented or fastidious. In graduate school he delivered a litter of poodles using a jelly knife that still had jelly on it.

The first year of my parents' separation he mastered shrimp and snow peas. He mastered Kung Pao chicken. I once came home to find a Peking duck drying over the stove on a hanger from the dry cleaner. Then there was the whole fish, glassy eyed and scaley, draped across the edges of his wok.

My father didn't start cooking for real until four years later when he moved from Brooklyn to New Hampshire. Soon he'd taught himself mousselines and pâtés, paella and risotto. He grew famous among his friends for his dinner parties, during which ambition, creativity, and flavor trumped presentation. The kitchen was a mess but the food usually wonderful.

His first horticultural project was a grow room in the basement of his house. The dank, sticky smell was overwhelming. He raised a dozen thriving plants—males and females standing off against large tinfoil backdrops—that he pollinated to perfection.

My father grew interested in Japanese gardening as he approached retirement. In 2019, he planted four Scots Pines around his pond in New Hampshire. He wanted to create something that would stand up and stand out against the harsh New England winters. The next year he hired someone to excavate forty-five red granite boulders from up the hill and place them around the pond.

When I told my father I was writing this, he asked me if you could see the boulders in the photo. I told him that I was writing about the garden reflected in the pond and not the garden itself. He sent me twenty additional photos of the garden and the pond, each one capturing something different—a seasonal change, a fresh bloom, and new tree. Just in case.

I'm not really writing about the garden, I said. Not like that. Not so that people will learn about Japanese gardening.

My father enrolled in an undergraduate Japanese class at Dartmouth. He took it twice. The captain of the football team was his classmate. He cooked Japanese food for the class at his farmhouse. He showed them the garden.

In 2019 my father traveled to Japan and toured some of the most world-famous gardens. This did not curtail his ambition. He returned and mastered Okonomiyaki—a messy and complicated Japanese pancake that sops up a hangover.

When my daughter was five, she fell in love with the garden. That's the summer this picture was taken. She has her own relationship with it, her own imaginary world. I'm not sure she appreciates the care and detail that goes into the pruning and placement of each tree. I'm not sure she understands how outlandish it is to have a celebrated Japanese garden in her grandfather's backyard in New Hampshire. She spends hours jumping from boulder to boulder, crossing the low bridge, raking the gravel. I don't ask her what is going through her head when she's out there, where her imagination takes her. That's for her to know.

A month after this photo was taken, my father called me from the hospital. He'd suffered an aortic aneurysm and said there was a fifty percent chance he wouldn't make it out of surgery. He told me how much he loved me and how wonderful my daughter is. He told me how much he loved seeing her play in the garden that summer and how much he wanted to see her do it again, but if he didn't, at least he'd experienced it for a few weeks of his life.

I have a photo of that day too—the day of the phone call. It is of me and a substitute postal worker crying on my porch. After years of trying, I'd given up attempting to befriend my usual surly mail carrier—a crabby man who preferred to leave the mail at the bottom of the steps of the driveway and not in the mailbox.

His replacement appeared in the early evening, way after the mail should have come, as I was getting off the phone with my father, perhaps for the last time. She heard my conversation and without asking, sat down next to me. That morning her cousin had been shot dead on the street in Inglewood. In the photo our eyes are swollen and red. But we are smiling. The next day the taciturn carrier resumed his route.

When my father came home from the rehab center (too quickly because he's an overachiever about most things) I forced him to walk out to the garden even though he didn't feel up to it. I put a chair out on the near side of the pond and encouraged him to reach it. I have a photo of this as well, but I don't like to look at it because I barely recognize the person sitting outside in bathrobe and holding a cane.

The day I flew home from that visit, my father called me to tell me he was already walking ten minutes unassisted. By the end of the week, he'd be up to twenty.

I tried to call my father just now to ask him a question about the garden, but he was out pruning. Perhaps he was up on a ladder or maybe wading in the pond. The spring is pruning season and by his own admission, he's working himself into a state of utter exhaustion. Which is a very good thing, he tells me. The amount of work that needs to be done is incomprehensible, he explains.

He would like you to know there are nearly one hundred and fifteen trees in the garden and that about sixty of them are conifers. He also would most likely tell you there are better pictures than the one above and that black and white doesn't really capture the majesty and the beauty of this improbable project. He's right but that's not the point.

When I float in his pond, the world turns upside down. I am inside the reflection—the trees and boulders made liquid—mutable and movable. This is my favorite view of the garden—look at it from below under the canopy of sky, where place and perspective are lost. Where the improbable becomes actual and I can reach below the surface and almost grab it.

MARA NASELLI
POWER LINES

To say this photograph was taken on a street halfway around the world presumes a *here*, where I am writing from, and a *there*, where I was. It was dusk, a short drive from a resort in a resort town where even a king could get away. The king hardly bears mentioning except by contrast. For non-kings, the beachside hotel and its movie-set grounds offer refuge: white beach, smiling staff to open your doors and nod with solicitude as you ask directions in the local language to the bathroom, pool, or buffet. By the beach, workers stayed up all night to manufacture a change in scenery for a three-day wedding other guests were instructed to avoid (the lawn, littered with spools of vinyl sheeting in a tropical pattern, half-constructed white and blue canopies, a splash of yellow flowers awaiting arrangement). Workers napped on the ground. A *here* and a *there*.

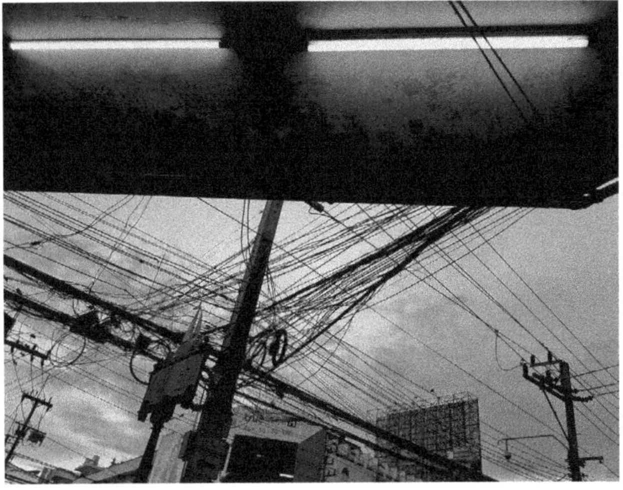

So one evening, to escape all that, we took our children down the road to a streetside restaurant, and something compelled me to look upward from under the drowsy awning sheltering diners from the equatorial sun.

I remember the crowded street—cars divided by red cement pilings and traffic stopped in one direction. Our pace slow and single file, we wound between tourists and restaurant tables edged to the curb in insistent invitation, with murky glass jars of chili oil and laminated menus worn gray from use. On the corner, a blue umbrella sheltered a woman selling salt-dried squid. At the next table, a man wearing a Pink Floyd t-shirt slung back in his chair, his young companion expressionless, her cold drink before her, its straw erect and untouched. I remember the moment I looked up into a tangle of phone and electrical wires—one technology on top of another, an unintentional architecture of the space, a different trace of our tracks.

The geographer Yi-Fu Tuan, who spent a lifetime studying how humans experience their environment, once noted that the invention of perspective in Renaissance painting tied the viewer to the distance represented as well as time. We measure distance and time together—it's a twenty-minute walk from here, a day's drive, a twelve-hour flight. When we look at a picture of a path moving away from us, we are looking into a future. What is behind us is the past.

I lived there decades ago, as a student, when I learned you could be sentenced to prison if you appeared to criticize the king. I wore my school uniform, flagged tuktuks, watched families sandwiched onto motorbikes weave through the blue haze of exhaust and stopped traffic. I observed the movement of shadows under the teak trees. I spoke with the house maid. I bowed before the Buddha. I bought sweet rice wrapped in banana leaves. The market smelled of persimmon, fish, and tamarind. Roaches scurried in the vendor's onion basket. Tiny red ants swarmed my bedsheets. On Thursday afternoons I taught meaningless words, like *flower, stitch,* and *purse,* to girls who had been forced into prostitution. Helpless against my students' impenetrable shyness, I faked an authority I didn't deserve—upbeat, undeterred. On my walks home, I understood the political posters papering the corrugated iron walls of the alleyway to be the tide of democracy, moving upward and onward into the future. That was then. This spring, a fifteen-year-old girl was one of eighteen children arrested for a peaceful protest against the law of lèse-magesté.

Perhaps I forgot the blue umbrella and the white man and his silent companion because I knew them to be ubiquitous, though I took pictures of both. What stayed with me, from this most recent visit, were the crisscrosses, flat planes, and glowing white bars of light in this photograph, its perspective unmoored, lines running from loops to vectors off the frame as an eyelid lowers on the aperture. It's a different vista from the beach and its infinite horizon beyond a foreground of vanished dirty plates and cocktail napkins. Different, too, from a home I visited thirty years ago, its courtyard studded with mango trees and orchids potted in coconut shells, where a young boy, the son of the servants, folded a piece of paper into an airplane and threw it into the sky.

JESSICA SILVESTER
THE FEAST OF SAN SILVERIO

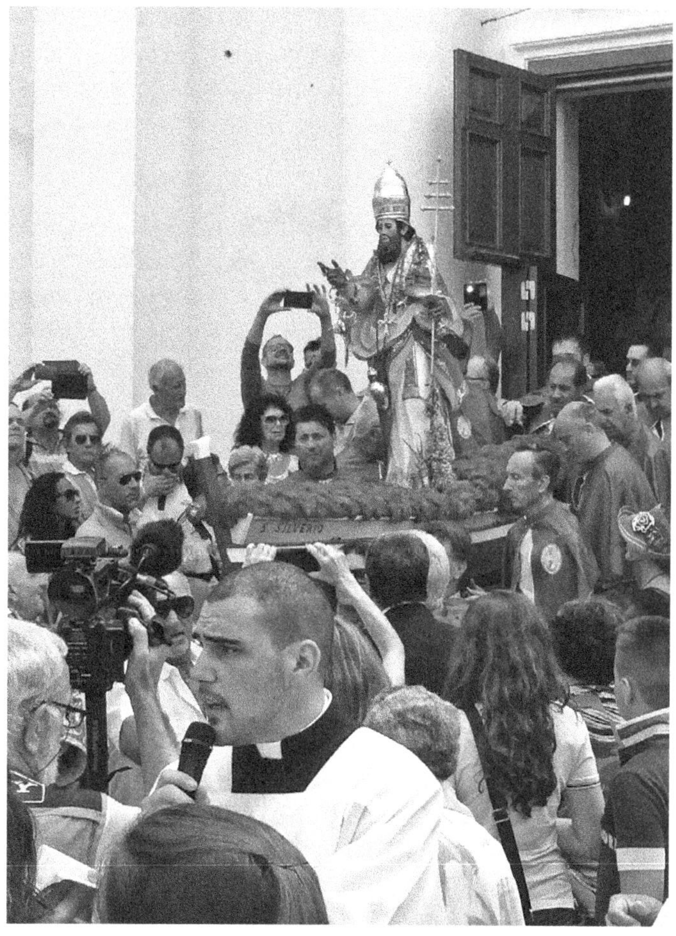

This priest. He's kind of . . . hot, isn't he? Why didn't I notice that at the time? Maybe I was too fixated on the outfits: one lady's purple pants, another's coral cotton-jersey dress, the many men in gold-horn necklaces catching the island's late-morning light. The heat was dizzying; the colors swirled: emerald-green Tyrrhenian Sea behind me; in front, a pastel yellow church centered by the crimson-and-gold statue of San Silverio, patron saint of Ponza.

Ponza. I can see the name of the island—my grandfather's birthplace—rising up through my mother's body. She stands in the kitchen of our two-bedroom house, a gravy-stained t-shirt skimming her breasts, her freckled legs liberated from the tweed pants she wore that day to teach middle school. She pronounces the word in one syllable, almost like a growl: *PAWNZ*. My *heritage*, she reminds me, raising a French manicured finger in the air like a gun and then aiming it straight between my eyes. She was always in the kitchen, and braless, when she told me important things.

In the old days, back in the Bronx, they had a San Silverio feast along Morris Avenue. It started on her block, 151st Street, where there was also the Ponzesi church, Our Lady of Pity, which was also where she attended Catholic School. She walked in the procession and ate *zeppoles* in her communion dress while the aunts all called after her: "Stay close, baby! Don't go too far!"

In this photo, my husband and I have come a very long way for the *real* festival in honor of the sixth-century pope, Silverio, who was falsely accused of treason and exiled to Ponza, where he died and was eventually sainted. He was not the only historical figure to be confined to the island, an ideal place for a jail, positioned as it was so far in the middle of nowhere—floating between Rome and Naples and 50 miles from any city (today, when a woman on the island goes into labor—which doesn't happen often considering its dwindling, largely elderly population of just a few thousand people—she might well wind up giving birth in mid-air, on the helicopter ride to Rome). The imperial Romans, the Bourbons, and the fascists all kept prisoners there; Mussolini himself became one of them after he was overthrown.

But on this day: Fireworks shot off the pier; carnations were tossed from balconies. "*Con Silverio*," we could hear people say to one another in passing. (No one speaks English on Ponza. Every time Dan and I visited—as we did again and again starting with our honeymoon—my Italian got a little better. I wanted to learn the language so badly. I never wanted to vacation anywhere else.)

Dan and I followed the Silverio statue in a procession through Ponza's cobblestone streets, trying to keep track of him until he eventually found his way onto a fishing boat in the harbor, the surrounding cliffs forming an amphitheater all around. We climbed aboard the dingy of a local fisherman named Paolo, who made some half-hearted attempts to point out Silverio's location amidst all the other boats in the harbor; I nodded and pretended to see him when I really did not. Paolo said that the fishermen prayed to Silverio to clear up storms. My mother didn't pray to him when she got cancer (everyone knows you go to Saint Anthony for that kind of miracle); still, she kept San Silverio medals in her mahogany jewelry drawer until the day she died.

I was on these waters with her once, on a family trip. At 14, I was just a few years younger than our guide, a blond, 1990s version of Paolo in neon orange trunks. Beside me on the bench seat, my mom glanced conspiratorially at me from behind her oval sunglasses as the wind caught his hair and the musk of his armpits caught my nostrils. We anchored in a blue grotto where the ancient Romans farmed moray eels; we stopped for lunch on a lava-hot rocky beach, where my cousins and I traded slightly different variations of prosciutto sandwiches, and my dad and uncle traded the camcorder to see who could get better footage of the topless women.

Now it was Dan beside me on the boat. He had an easier time than I keeping his sights on San Silverio. "He was right behind me!" Dan would say. "Oop, there he is again!" It became a running joke. Like a Where's Waldo game. I giggled, but I couldn't fully surrender my seriousness. I so badly wanted the San Silverio shrine to be majestic, or even just well painted. I didn't want it to be, essentially, the Roaming Gnome from those Travelocity commercials.

But my mother, I think, would've been able to see it both ways: the gravity of the proceedings and the levity, too. That was just how she was, as quick to bow her head in prayer as to double over in laughter. Was she born that way? Did she become herself over time? Maybe when you're a girl from the Bronx—never allowed to stray very far, in or out of your communion dress—you find that range within yourself so as to feel less stuck in one place; or, at the very least, you learn to appreciate cheap thrills.

LYNELL GEORGE
OFF MAP

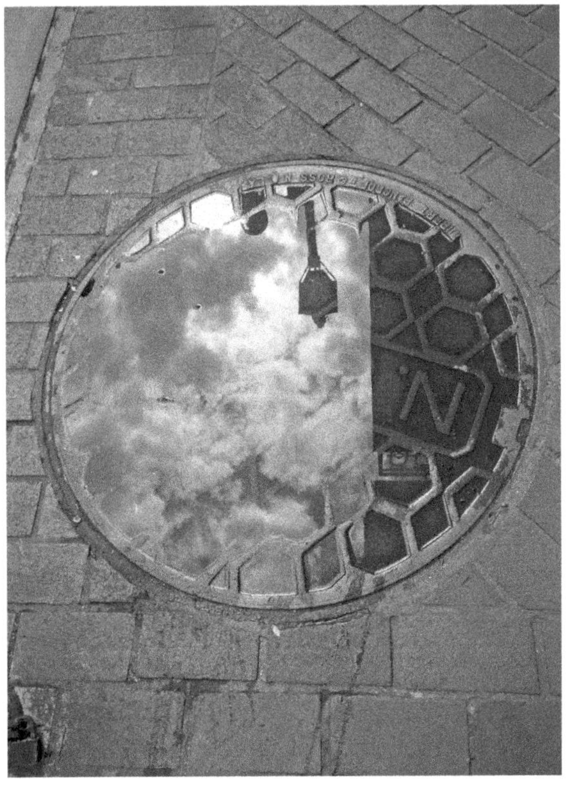

Shuffling through a messy set of my New Orleans photographs, I discern a truth: I'm preoccupied with doors that lead to nowhere. Broken entryway buzzers. Cement-sealed mail chutes. Illegible street markers. Quick-sketch, graffitied stand-ins for the thing itself: a ghost window sketched upon a sidewalk, a spray-painted door knob on a brick wall. New Orleans, my ancestral home, is host to an abundance of these commentaries. Moments that seem to speak to the city's ability to take something inconvenient or absurd and turn it into an open question, a story.

My eye is calibrated precisely for this sort of non-sequitur, a playfulness that pushes back. I come from people whose sense of humor has been cultivated as a tool of survival, coping: Quick. Wry. Sharp. "*You can't get that past me.*" We are saying several things at once, behind our smile and wink. We are rewriting, correcting, improvising. We are trading in code, in our ancient, nested talk. And though all of them—my grands and great-grands, aunts and uncles, the cousins, "play" and real—are gone from this place, I carry them close.

These snapshots carry me across a threshold. They collapse time: Before this set of photographs, it had been twenty years, at least, since my last visit to New Orleans. The visit was strictly a reporting and research journey, intentionally brief—hours not days—a swift boomerang back to California, Thanksgiving day. The *why* of that, I'm still parsing. It is separate subject matter from the newspaper piece, a profile of a New Orleans culture bearer, for which I've traveled to collect color and quotes. I push *feeling* aside. I concentrate on tasks.

At the front desk, I ask if there might be a preferred, or picturesque, route to walk to my interview. I want to get my bearings, catch up on lost time. When the concierge—a Black man who looks like kin especially around the eyes—tells me: "Miss Lynell, that destination is off the map." I know to read both around and *into* his words. His response is both literal and a metaphor. He slides the hotel's paper "courtesy map" closer, leans over and with his pen, draws a brief squiggle down Chartres Street. The line connects nothing to nothing. it floats between here and there, between present and future. Just as I do at this moment.

Without saying outright, the concierge gracefully attempts to convey that, in terms of a stroll, it's best to stay *on* the map. He will not direct me otherwise. I am trying to convey to this gentle man, also without saying outright, that, even though I'm occupying in this lavish French Quarter hotel, ornate as a wedding cake, conversing over a courtesy map full of abbreviated streets, abbreviated possibilities and, accordingly, abbreviated consequences, I am not a tourist.

Though California-born, how to express that my soul is here? Somewhere.

Before this stay, I'd never before contemplated hotel lodgings in New Orleans. Storied Jim Crow legacies of exclusion aside, I never thought I would need to. For most of my life, there was always family, *off* this map. An abundance of them. Then more around the corner. Walkable, if it wasn't in the midst of the dead-weight heat of summer. But now, I am without those back-pocket addresses. Hurricane Katrina and the aftermath took the last of those. Scattered and resettled them. Still, I am no one's tourist. I know the history, the stories, but these are the new circumstances, and I have pressing, present-tense work to do.

If I let them—the doormen, the bellhops, the concierge, the women who float in to turn down my bed linen in the evening, and leave me extra bottles of fancy water in the mini-fridge—they are there to serve as my family. Royce and Gerald and "Big Kevin"—all of them, already, issuing directives, warnings, advice: "Don't walk below St. Ann real late night or early in the morning. People still carryin' on . . ." "Slow down." " "Don't be so serious. Have some fun."

The family I am mourning, whom I will forever mourn, have sent down some sort of advisory, clearly: "Someone please look out for this hard-headed child . . . ."

I acquiesce. I board the cab that Royce the doorman has hailed at the concierge's behest. I deliver my most polite I-have-home-training "thank yous." On the short ride to the Marigny, I take in the architectural flourishes, the large graffitied double-entendre testimonies ("You Deserve to Be Here . . ."), the kudzu overtaking the forlorn addresses, centuries-old storm-ravaged buildings, still struggling back from nature and once again succumbing to it.

Despite my efforts to not get distracted by emotions, I feel a shiver move through my body. The whole of it: the fullness and the loss. I realize that I'm trying to climb into a feeling. This is a process of reclamation, a broken lock I'm trying to pick.

When we arrive at the "off-the-map" destination, the address I've scrawled, perhaps too-quickly, into my reporter's notebook, the building looks as if it is shuttered tight. Not just for the night, but abandoned, awaiting its kudzu takeover. The cab driver isn't sure himself, and tells me that he'll make a loop just to play it safe. Before he is fully out of sight, I hear my name, rather an echo of it, the final syllable ringing in the heavy air, then the figure attached to the voice appears. My interview subject, unhurried. He extends the unexpected: An embrace. A warm cup of coffee pressed into my hands. We match our gaits. Without asking he seems to understand that I need to get back "home." We walk. We sidestep small talk. We go into the marrow. We sink into the marshy, fraught history of this place. I train my camera. We cross the railroad tracks at the site where in 1890 Homer Plessy refused to sit in the "Colored" car. We wind through a stretch of cottages still tattooed with "Katrina Crosses"—the spray-painted X-codes painted by FEMA workers in 2005 to identify rescue priorities after the flood. This is the real work. The rest will find its way in. It must.

This is re-syncing and reclaiming. There is no snapshot of this moment, but I still feel it in my body.

So much of my being belongs to this place.

I wish I had a frame, just one. An image that stops time. A single frame that denotes the epiphany, the inside turned outside, made legible. Not the sly rejoinder. Not a false doorway or a staircase that leads nowhere, but a portal, real and true, that opens onto a new chapter, that reveals not things as they are, but as they should be.

Maybe it's a transformation still evolving, slowly, steadily: a subtle image materializing within emulsion, capturing that exact, discrete instance when I knew that I was back, or rather, that I'd never been far away at all.

STUART DYBEK
BACKCOUNTRY

The birds that lifted and circled complaining as we arrived had resettled in the guano-splattered trees. In the undercut beneath the overhanging mangroves, the water at high tide was clear and deep enough to spearfish. I snorkeled among tangled roots, careful not snag my net catch bag. It was weighted with tonight's dinner, two snappers. I wanted one more fish, to make a ceviche for tomorrow's breakfast.

Three days of small craft warnings had left me hungry for fish fresh out of the water. I'd slept restlessly to wind soughing and woke to a pitching, white-capped Atlantic. It was the last week of the annual fishing trip that a buddy and I began taking after he'd asked, "Think we'll get around to fishing before they have to wheel us to the shore?"

Rather than wait out the wind, we decided to find shelter from it on the Gulf side, which afforded some lee. Keys locals call the Atlantic side "Out Front." The Gulf side is the backcountry, an archipelago of uninhabitable mangrove keys, rookeries for waterbirds: cormorants, heron, pelicans, kingfishers, osprey. The shallow, shoaly water makes it one of the richest fish nurseries on the planet. We hired an old friend, Bill, a guide with a flat-bottomed Carolina skiff, that now was anchored forty yards off Crawl Key. The name perhaps refers to turtle kraals from an era when Key West had an unregulated turtle trade. The backcountry remains unspoiled enough to sense ghosts from when leatherback turtles were endangered. The ocean remains one of the last true wildernesses left on a planet threatened by climate change. By simply wearing a dive mask and plunging your face underwater you'll see an authentically wild world living by its own rules.

Within the labyrinthine tangle of mangrove roots, clouds of silversides glittered like fish confetti. There wasn't a reef, but reef fish were there—sergeant majors, angels, grunts, giant electric blue parrot fish. There were snook, and resident groupers, barracuda, sting rays, visiting schools of spade fish and jacks. Mangrove snapper, a sustainable species, schooled in the hundreds. I'd taken two keepers, which I'd killed immediately, so that they wouldn't suffer, and as a precaution. Like blood in the water, the flopping of a wounded fish attracts sharks.

A shark mention early in a story brings to mind what's known as Chekhov's gun, a dramatic principle, which says that if the gun is not going to be fired in the third act, then it shouldn't be there in the first. But sharks, unlike guns, are part of the natural order. Mentioned or not, they're there, aware of you. Their lateral lines detect the faintest vibration in the water. They can sense a drop of blood from a third of a mile away.

As a kid in inner-city Chicago, I learned to swim and later to scuba in Lake Michigan. In my mid-twenties, I left the city to teach for two years at a local junior high in the Caribbean. It's where I learned to spearfish, and first encountered sharks: two twelve-foot tigers, among the largest I've seen, slowly gliding by, ravening eyes aware, but disinterested. The moment left a lasting realization, no less elemental for being obvious, that despite how intense one's love of ocean, we're not designed for it. The mammals that have successfully returned to the sea don't need to shop for fins. If a large shark wanted you, there's little you could do about it.

The legal size for keeping a mangrove snapper is ten inches. I was after a larger fish, with the heft of those in my bag. I floated above the snappers that swam in and out of the cover of roots. The bigger ones spooked easily. I presumed they all were feeding. Feeding is why fish strike baits, and yet I'd seldom witnessed snappers striking the silversides, or a barracuda taking a snapper, as if doing so would disrupt the dreamy, almost hypnotic rhythm of life in the undercut.

Instead of a photo of fish, I've chosen a shot of a catch bag. In black and white the nylon bag looks almost like an abstract form. Its actual color is iridescent green, which makes it easier to spot if lost. A still photo of the fish on the day I'm describing can't convey the sensation I'd like to recreate. I would have needed to be holding an underwater movie camera, instead of a speargun, for that.

Envision yourself alone on a narrow, city street with a park at one end whose trees blaze from within with the force that throws light rather than shade. Without warning, a silent implosion of energy swirls and scatters mounds of leaves along the gutters in what's suddenly become a wind tunnel, one in which you are the only inaction. Leaves sweep at you, then by you, leaving you untouched.

The street, of course, is the undercut trench, and the leaves are fish, seemingly thousands, fish of all kinds and colors sweeping past, a single, fragmented school, with no more sense of agency than that of dry leaves in October. A dive mask with its lack of peripheral vision, prevents whipping your head around as they gust past. Every move you make in water is slo-mo. When you do turn, they're gone, vanished, leaving the trench beneath the mangroves that teemed with life, empty. And then you see the wind coming as if to catch up with what it has blown away. The wind is a bull shark.

The shark is oversized for the undercut we now share. When it sees me holding the game bag that has guided it here, it stops as if braking and appears surprised. (Memory doesn't edit out anthropomorphisms.) We're in a stare down.

Long ago in the Caribbean, after a day of parent-teacher conferences had left me with an appetite for the reward of a fresh fish for dinner, I snorkeled to a reef offshore, fully aware I was breaking the rules: 1) diving alone, 2) at twilight, 3) with a catch bag attached to my weight belt after taking a fish. A reef shark, barely four feet, maybe still a juvenile appeared. I wasn't alarmed until it began to circle, vigorously swishing its tail so that its entire body twisted as if doing a shark dance. First, I floated quietly in place, then I shouted at it underwater, but the circles just got tighter, and the dance wilder. And it was getting darker. With my gun extended like the spear on a billfish, I swam directly at it, and it whirled and disappeared nearly too fast for the eye to follow.

The bull shark whirled when I swam at it, but the space was too narrow and mud puffed up as I watched the girth and length of the shark unfurl. I knew from the size of its head that it was large, but not until it struggled to turn did I realize it was a nine-foot fish. One that thankfully was gone. Fishing was over, but before I could start across the shallow water for the boat, the shark was back, parked closer to me this time. I swam at it again and it turned, more slowly, as if giving me a longer look at what I was dealing with, before its tailfin wagged off in the wake of suspended mud.

I knew it would be back. It made me uneasy taking my eyes off the underwater trench for even the moments it took to reach as high as I could and loop the draw string of my catch bag around the branch of an overhanging mangrove. The green bag sagging with fish hung dripping just above the surface, and I slid under and started for the boat. It seemed a long swim as I repeatedly stopped to turn and check whether I was being followed, and to scan the surface for a fin, aware that bull sharks are infamous for attacks in shallow water.

We motored back to retrieve the fish for dinner. The catch bag's iridescence was easy to spot among the trees. The water was losing clarity as the tide fell, and even with the engine raised, the boat had to stop just short of the mangroves. There was no sight of the shark. I slipped back into the water, swam the few strokes to the bag, and reached to unloop the draw string, expecting the weight of the snappers. Instead, the bag collapsed in on itself, empty. None of us had seen the sight of the shark surging up and ripping the bottom out as it splashed back. I kept the bag, thinking that besides taking its picture, someday I might mount it, spread out with its torn bottom reshaped by the ragged imprint of hunger.

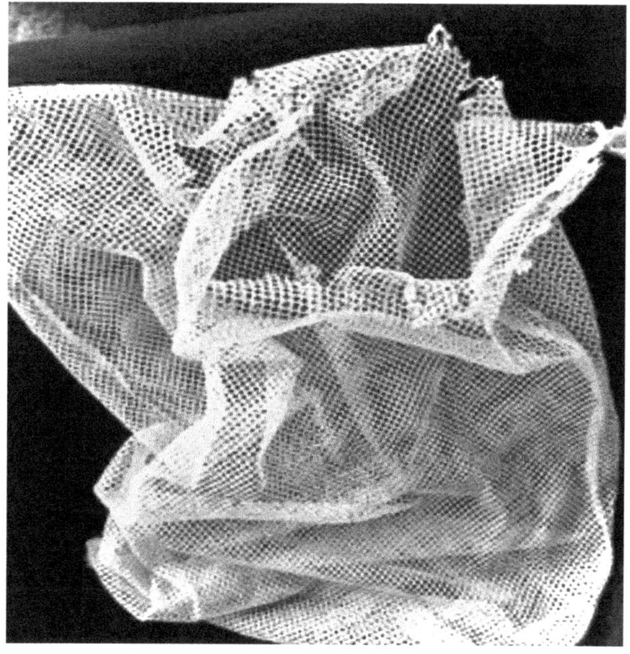

5 BEFORE AND AFTER

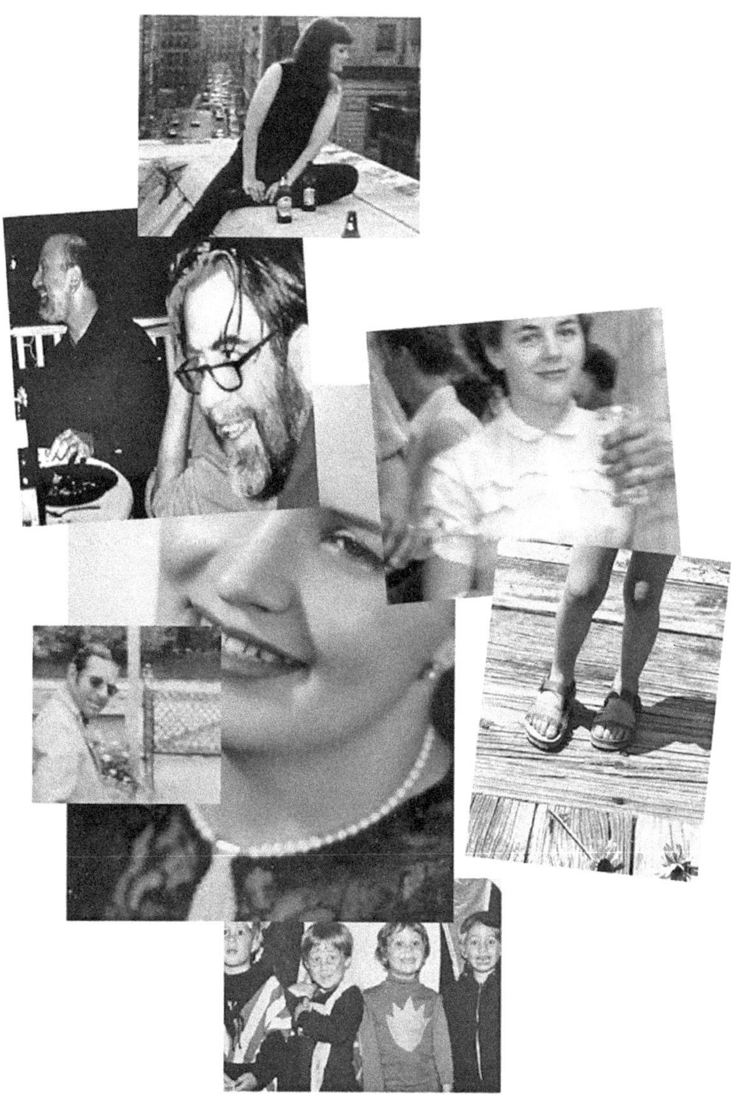

"At that dock, in the sunlight, I had no idea we were at the end of something—"

LESLIE JAMISON

SUSAN STRAIGHT
RICHARD AND GABRIELLE STRAIGHT

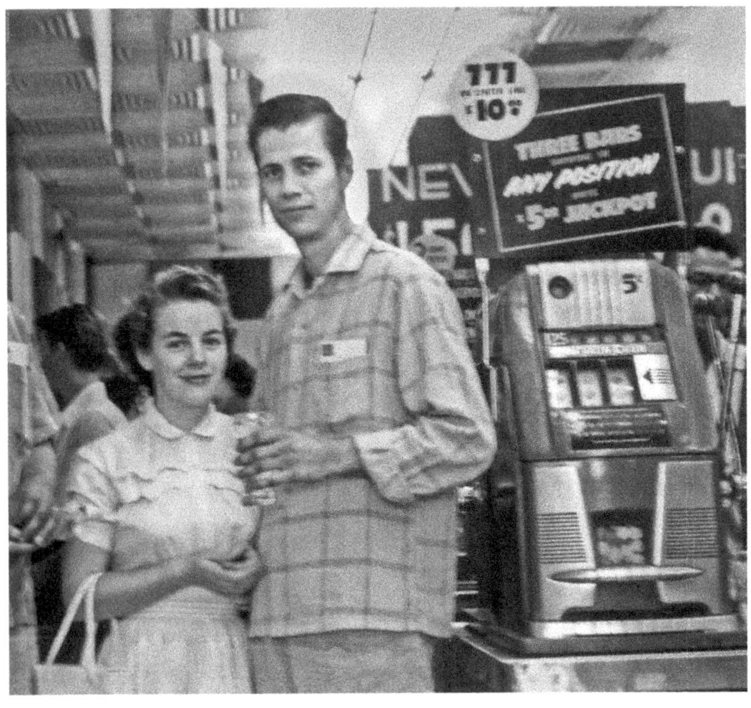

I never saw this image of my parents, taken in Las Vegas by a casino photographer who then sent this as a postcard to the young couple, until I was an adult.

My mother kept it in a small homemade photo album, the kind I imagine was sold in the 1950s. The covers are two soft brown pieces of suede. The front piece is tooled with “Photos Yosemite Nat’l Park”, and a hand-painted illustration of a pine branch and cone. Three holes punched into the leather, like I used to punch holes in hand-tooled leather belts we were taught to make at the YWCA, where my mother took me as a child. My mother has tied the album covers together with cream-colored yarn, three strands.

I assume she bought it when my father took her to Yosemite, before I was born. They went to San Francisco and saw the Dodgers play. They fed a deer. They saw the ocean at Carmel. These black and white Kodak photos are fastened on the black felt pages of the album by creamy paper corners. The snapshots are scalloped around the edges. My mother has written the location and a funny note in white ink for each image.

There are 82 photos, from November 1955, when I assume they got married, featuring their vacations to Sequoia and San Diego. There are a few photos of my mother's grandparents in Switzerland, mailed to her, and my father's father and stepmother visiting from their ranch in Colorado. A few photos of my father with his young son and daughter from his first marriage, when he was nineteen, and his sister and her second husband. A few of his friends. One of my mother working behind the counter at Household Finance, the loan company where she was a teller, which is how she met Richard Straight. He was sleeping in his car, on strike from the Boeing Aircraft plant in Riverside where he worked on the assembly line but had big ideas for new parts for the planes. He needed $50 to survive. She got him the loan. He asked her out. She agreed.

This image, in Las Vegas, is from July 1956. They look like who they are, to me, when I study it now. My mother five feet tall, dressed conservatively, with not much money (but she could sew), looking a little nervous, probably about money. My father six feet tall, dressed like a guy on vacation from his travelling salesman job, where he delivers cigarettes and alcohol to bars, gas stations, hotels, and liquor stores, stocking the cigarette machines, smoking his own Tareyton brand. He looks nervous, too, probably about money.

Maybe they should never have gone on a date, or gotten married. They both had terrible childhoods, in different ways, and felt as if the world owed them more, and they couldn't quite get it.

*

She was born in the high mountains of Switzerland, the Berner Oberland Alps, in a tiny village. She learned to knit when she was five. She darned socks for her father and brothers, as did all little Swiss girls. She had a basket to collect apples and pears. She wore an apron over her dress. She went to the woods with the basket over her arm. I have seen a single photo of her young childhood and it is that image. Her hair is braided.

Her mother died when she was nine, her brothers were younger, and her father married the nurse who had cared for her mother on her sickbed, as was said back then, in 1943. My mother, Gabrielle Gertrude Leu, was forever then the bad stepdaughter. She leaned into it.

Eventually, her father took the family from that Swiss mountain on a boat to Ontario, Canada, where my mother worked in corn and strawberry fields, at fifteen. She couldn't go to school—that was for the younger siblings, including her new half-sister. Eventually, at fifteen, my mother ran away, with her single suitcase, to the town of Oshawa, and got a job as an au pair.

The family left Canada for America, first the agricultural fields of Florida, and finally, in a travel trailer, arrived in Fontana, California, where my stepgrandmother, Rose, had seen an advertisement on a postcard. Snow-covered mountains behind trees laden with oranges. Nurses hired immediately at Kaiser Steel Company. She was hired immediately. The family settled into a trailer park, in the travel trailer.

My mother waited until she was nineteen to join them. She crossed the border with a visa, and lasted three days in the trailer, she always said. She wanted a real house. She took that suitcase and went to a rented room in Riverside, California, ten miles away, and got a job at Household Finance.

*

My father was born in the Rocky Mountains of Colorado, and lived on an isolated ranch in Fraser, the coldest place in America. His father was violent, a rancher and gunman who had his own hard time as the eldest of ten kids in the early 1900s. My father was the youngest of four kids, his sister died of a heart defect in front of him, and he was rounding up sheep in the mountains when he was eight, riding a white horse alone through deserted pastures. The gates. Close the gate. When he was 86, his memory failing, his voicemail said, "Don't forget to close the gate."

My father was haunted. In the hospital, I sat beside him, his feet bare and painful, a legacy of standing for hours in a half-frozen creek hauling Christmas trees they'd cut down in the forest to sell, his father shouting they had to get to town.

*

They went to Vegas in July 1956, and a casino photographer captured this image, and they paid a few dollars, and he mailed it to the little wooden back house where they lived, on Tyrolite Street in Glen Avon, California, an unincorporated community known as Okie Town. My father had come to nearby Ontario, California, when he was nine, the first of many times his mother fled brutal violence on the ranch. He and his mother went back and forth many times, to the Rockies, then to Ontario, and finally, when he was fifteen, his father beat him and his mother, and left. His mother left, too, for his father. Richard Straight slept in the kitchen of a Foster Freeze, never went back to school, and joined the military at seventeen.

I have no idea what they talked about, my parents, here in Vegas, in the little shack on Tyrolite, whether they shared stories about all they hadn't been able to do, but my mother wanted one thing: a house. Her own house. With a yard. By October 1960, they had a one-bedroom house off Pyrite Street, a mile away. They owned it. My mother was elated. A few months later, there is a photo of me, in the center of a black felt page, my hands up like I'm getting arrested, though I'm lying on my back, of course. My mother has written in white ink: *The new Chapter in our Life*, and my name. To the right of me, the words: *Here she is one day old!* To the left of me: *For picture of Happy Father, see over*

On the back of that black felt page, a photo of my father, in a liquor store somewhere in the desert, working on the day I was born. *The Happy Father—Holding a Store Sale.* There are thirty more photos in this soft album, which I handle so carefully because until three years ago, I had only glimpsed it. My mother has about fifteen photo albums, but this one was hidden away. She has severe memory loss now, and we had to move her to an assisted living apartment a mile from my house, and I see her almost every day. My fierce little mother. I have her sewing machine, her knitting needles, and this album. We sit at the table in my kitchen, the first dining room table she ever bought. Maple. From the 1960s. We play

Rummikub and eat Swiss chocolate from her childhood. I would never show her this photo album, and never this snapshot.

There are thirty images after I am born—the house of which she was so proud, a station wagon, her yard, her fence, her roses, her cats, and me in a jumper, a walker, a stroller, a Radio Flyer wagon, and finally, a tricycle. I am about two. She is not in the images. She is taking the photos. My father is gone. He left the month after I turned three, and she was eight months pregnant. The final two snapshots are color, faded—Trying to Be Funny, my mother has written in white ink, and I am holding my arms up, sitting on a tiny table near the TV trays with butterflies I remember so vividly, and Mopsy, a cat, sitting in a rocking chair. There are three black felt pages left, all blank.

SVEN BIRKERTS
FIFTY

The structure is circular, moving clockwise around the faces, sparking the criss-cross of eye-beams. The photo tells of a particular time. Historically, it's ten days after the World Trade Center attacks, though the festive air around the table—the occasion is my 50th birthday—would seem to belie that, but that larger awareness has become part of my looking.

My first response is neither aesthetic nor historical. I take in the image as a whole, but what I register right away is a quick poignant stab. Never fails. My eye goes straight to Liam Rector, the bearded man on the right.

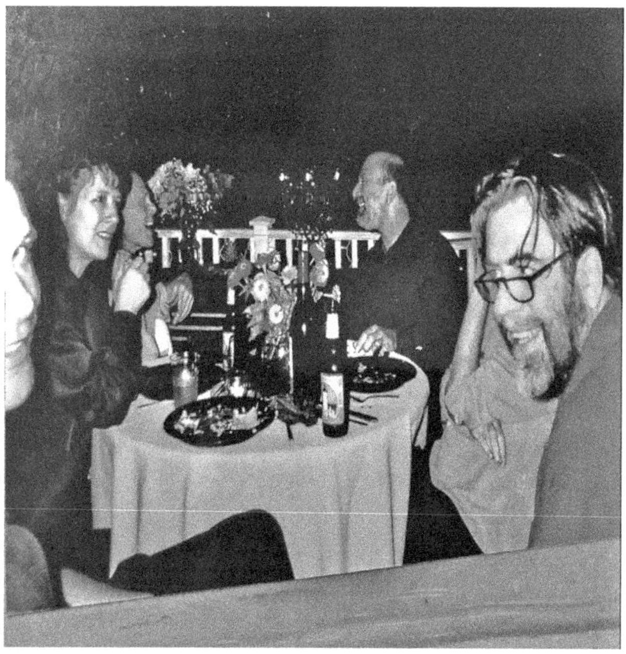

Liam was at that time the Director of the Bennington Writing Seminars—my boss, though the word doesn't sit right because he was also a friend. I did work for Liam, teaching nonfiction workshops in the winter and summer residencies, but those contacts were more professional than personal. Our friendship happened away from the campus, mostly around Boston and New York, as with the semester I was invited to give a course at the New School.

I would take the train from Boston to New York one day a week, teach my evening class, and then walk the few short blocks to Liam and Tree's apartment (Tree Swenson, Liam's wife, is the woman on the other side of the table). These nights, maybe a dozen of them, were occasions unto themselves.

Liam would open the door almost before I rang and would then go straight to the kitchen to get drinks. He was hungry for talk—it was obvious. He would sit at the edge of the long couch, leaning forward. He was a big, bearded man, with glowering eyebrows, an enthusiast, and I felt the weight of his full attention.

Addressing me as friend and confidant, Liam would cover the waterfront. He would vent, ask advice, strategize, gossip. He loved gossip. As soon as I offered even the smallest crumb of news, he started to probe. Insist. "What else, Sven?" He was a person—there are a few—who I could not bear to disappoint. I would dig deeper, give out more details. Later, I sometimes wondered if I had said too much. There was that impulse to call and say, "That thing I mentioned . . . ."

At some point—without fail—Liam would put his hands on his knees and say "Let's go into my study." It was late by then and Tree would have long retired. He had to play me this song, and this, and this; it was one of his obsessions—he always had another song I had to hear. One night it was Eva Cassidy's "Fields of Gold." He told me had heard it first waiting in line at the post office. "Sven, I started to cry."

That's the backdrop, the partial context. My visceral memory flash is of sitting almost knee to knee with Liam in that room and making myself respond to every song he played, knowing it would not be good to say I was tired. I still see Liam in his swivel chair, leaning forward, eyebrows raised, waiting for my reaction.

Seven years later, Liam would without any warning take his life. It was a blow. Why? Does anyone really ever know? I think of Liam often, those long New York nights, the eagerness with which he opened his door.

*

The party photo holds so much more. It's almost as if one transparency—one layer of time—were laid atop another. Now, twenty years later, I can't not register the various fates and outcomes.

One outcome, profound for me, was that after Liam's death, I became director of his program. I put in ten years on top of the ten I'd already logged as a member of his faculty. It was just five years ago that I finally stepped down.

Tree, widowed, moved to Seattle and for years directed Hugo House, an arts organization. The writer Doug Bauer, sitting behind her, still teaches in the program twenty-some years later.

Doug is talking with the painter Gerry Bergstein, who I barely knew at the time but who has now become a close friend—a happy development that I can't now unsee. Pausing on Gerry's face, I get the image—and sensation—from visiting him a few years ago in his studio. It was several narrow stairways up in an old building in Boston: dense spatter of paint on the tarps on the floor, jars with brushes, a palette, tubes of paint everywhere, each banded with a different stripe of color. I look at Gerry in the photo and I see the seated man, but I also see the artist in his world.

Finally, Chris Benfey, the merest slice of his presence on the far left. Chris and I taught at Mt. Holyoke College in the late 1980s. We began to correspond after I left and met up several times a year for walks. More recently, we carried on a year-long exchange on the idea of serendipity.

And then serendipity prevailed. For less than two years ago, my wife Lynn and I felt it was time to move from Arlington, our home of thirty-some years. We searched here and there and finally found the house we wanted in Amherst, where we live less than two miles from Chris and Mickey, his wife.

The party photo, taken on the last day of summer, has become a kind of talisman, holding so much of my life in its four corners, that massive compression of time embedded in a moment forever frozen, memento and harbinger both.

ADRIANA E. RAMIREZ
FINITA

I am not close with my father's side of the family.

This is only true in the present tense. In the past, I would have been lying. But the past is always a lie of imagination belying any sense of control we have over the whole endeavor.

I am not close with my father's side of the family. That should be enough.

Like all human beings, though, I am the architect of my own demise, forever evoking that which I have pledged to forget. I hung up her photograph in my library. I gave my daughter her name—not just her name, but also her nickname. She is in the parts of my face that someone once called *striking*, so I carry her—grand-filial guilt and all.

What is it, *to grandmother*? Is it an apology? An opportunity to love without stakes?

As a child, I saw her as impossibly old. And now that I'm closer to her age at that time than I am to being a child, I cannot help but reconsider my own mortal looks: Will I too become impossibly old? Will I also be forgiven too late, left hanging on a burgundy-painted wall?

At least I picked the good picture. The one where she's about to turn twenty-five, about to get married for the second time, right after she found my grandfather, a new father for her three small boys. It's not her fault it took me so long to humanize her. (I had to have my own children first.)

I used to be close with her, my father's mother, my grandmother Josefina.
I used to love her most of all.

At her funeral, my father asked me to speak. I got up, as I always do at family functions, public speaker that I am. He'd just finished eulogizing her, and I although I was not sure I wanted to follow his emotional and scattered speech, I felt like I had to stand up when he called upon me. I looked at everyone gathered before me. Only a few really knew my grandmother, family mostly. The rest were there to support us, out of respect for my father and his sisters, his brothers notably absent.

My father's family is a Mexican gothic novel, spanning decades and continents, with loves and betrayals and weird secrets, and all of them bear their tragedies nobly, mostly through deep artistic expression and alcoholism. My father (who rarely drinks) and his siblings (who drink voraciously) can all sing and play instruments, something they got from her. Not that I ever heard her voice—all I heard was the rasp of tequila and time.

"She taught me to love flowers," I began. She did teach me to love flowers, so it seemed like a good way to start my three minutes on the things I'd loved about her. But in the moment, my brain went all Proust and suddenly I saw her, tending to her roses and her lilies, telling me the names of all the flowers, teaching me to make my own perfume, holding my eight-year-old hand as we carefully picked our way through her garden.

I didn't say anything else at the funeral. The sob caught in the throat. "She taught me to love flowers," I repeated before I sat down. I cry ugly and I preferred few people witness the flood of emotion catching me by surprise.

I had not said goodbye to her when she was dying. I could not afford the trip and I was in love with the man I would eventually marry, investing in all the right things at the wrong times. We'd become occasional penpals, my grandmother and I, after I enforced radio silence, decades after she taught me the difference between a day lily and a calla lily.

Years after my only brother died, when I was about sixteen years old, my grandmother lied to me about why my parents never had another child. She and I would stay up talking during super long sleepovers in her room, identical twin beds on opposite sides under opposite windows. I told her everything, how his absence had shaped my childhood, and she listened. And then, one day, out of the blue, she said that my parents had lied to me: They could have had another child and simply chose not to.

For days, I processed that. My brother had died a decade earlier, and I imagined what it would have been like to have a sibling. Why, I wondered, hadn't my parents tried again? I had vague recollections of them promising a new sibling, then telling me it wasn't on the cards. I never even considered that they hadn't told the truth.

When I confronted her, my infuriated mother clarified the effects of her uterine cancer on both conceiving a child and adoption; slowly, I extinguished a resentment that had not lived long enough be named. It was my grandmother who had lied. About something that mattered. For no reason at all. She was the first person I stopped speaking to. I began referring to her in past tense long before she died.

She wasn't the type of woman who would apologize to a child. I know this about her. I remember she had a typewriter in her hallway that no one was allowed to touch. As a child, of course I pressed its buttons every chance I got. Once, she caught me, and laughed, pressing all the keys with me. Then she turned, grabbed a ruler, and whacked my knuckles for every letter of the alphabet. Now, raising my own kids, I think about how much I bend, and how little she ever could.

Still, she understood my silence. She never asked me what happened, why I turned from her. She knew. But what was there to say? Her grief was a form of madness; mine was silent.

There are betrayals that live in the heart, that take root and become great trees, fed on resentment and bound in the enshrined caprice of childhood. I did not forgive my grandmother until I cried at her funeral.

I had not visited her as she died. I kissed a boy instead. I married him and planted day lilies in my garden, grew some life of my own: little ones with striking faces and too many questions about the beautiful woman who hangs on the wall in the library.

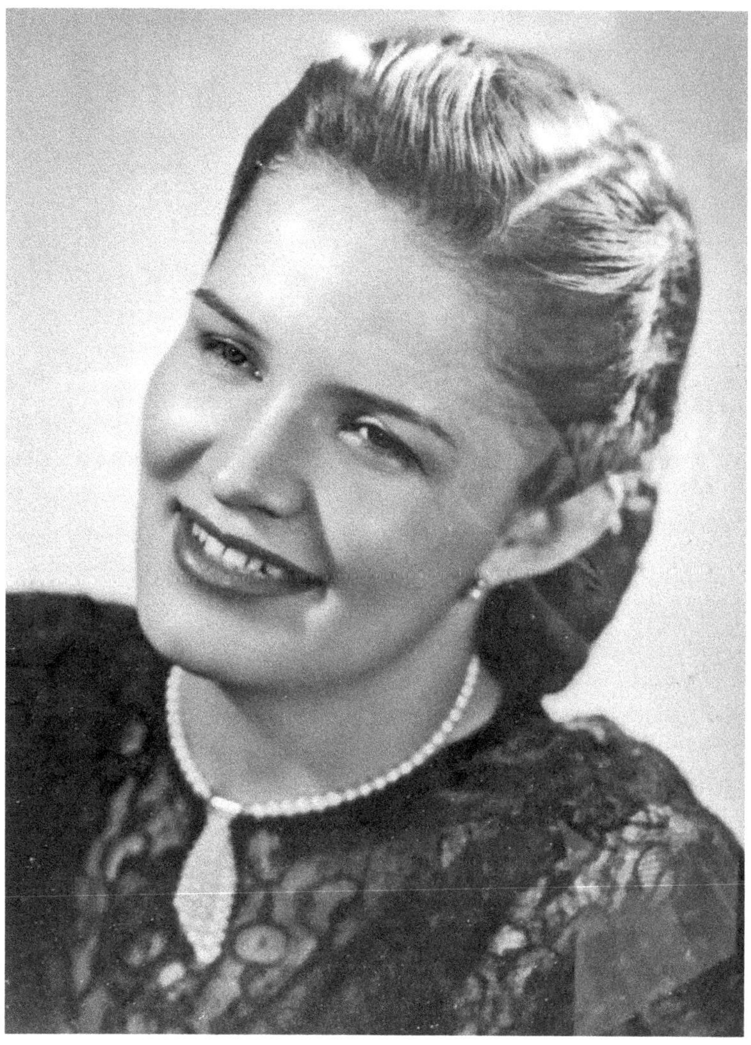

"She was a princess," my daughter says.
"She's dead now," says my son. "Am I right?"

I am not close with my father's side of the family. Not anymore anyway.

DIANA WAGMAN
TRICK OR TREAT

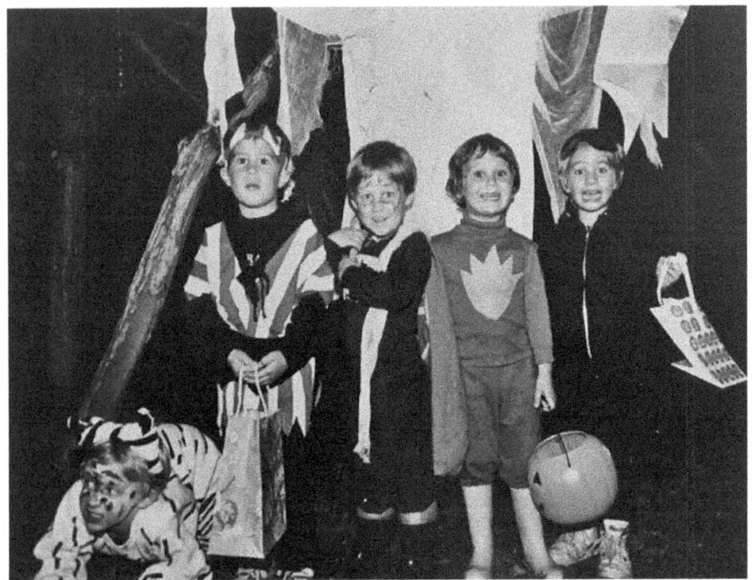

Photo credit: Tod Mesirow

Halloween. It was the favorite holiday in our house when our children were young. No family obligations, just costumes and candy and the chance to stay out after dark. The discussions of who or what to be would start in August. The collecting of costume pieces and accouterments, borrowing boots and hats, making wings or ears made for great times we spent together. The costumes were always homemade and I am not a seamstress—double stick tape, staples, some big sloppy stitches held them together.

My son danced around me, his fingers trembled and tapped the old shirt as I glued and cut. Hurry, hurry, hurry. He was four years old and had chosen to be a mostly unknown cartoon bear—SuperTed. Trying on his costume he was so excited I worried he'd cry. He was thrilled with the result: yellow rain boots, red sweatpants, a red turtleneck from the thrift store augmented with a yellow felt symbol I'd pasted on. And a cape of course.

With him in the photo are a tiger and a snake charmer (brothers), a pirate, and his friend Nick, dressed all in black. A ninja? Five blond boys, privileged, adored, each born in perfection; hearts, minds, and bodies healthy and intact. They have every advantage. The tiger looks to his right at some unseen prey. He snarls, ready to attack. The pirate looks beyond the camera. To the next house? To the one that gives out peanut butter cups? Or to his future?

Halloween. It marks the end of summer and the beginning of the dark, cold winter. Many believe it is the day when the boundary between the realms of the living and the dead is at its thinnest, a mere translucent mist. The people of the past can step through to stand beside you. The Celts wore costumes so the ghosts wouldn't recognize them and they could avoid any unfinished business, grudges, or feuds. In Mexico they build altars and offer their ancestors their favorite foods to eat and drink together. In Italy, it's called Ognissanti and celebrants leave a full pitcher of water on the kitchen table for the dead to drink when they visit.

These five boys only want candy and the chance to run around with their friends at night. It is not the past they have to worry about—they have no past, no ghosts to spook them—but the future . . . What will happen to them? Where will they end up? Will they achieve their potential? I remember that word as it related to little-girl me. It was said I had so much potential. Ten years later, I wasn't performing up to potential. Fifteen years later I had wasted my potential. And I have lived with that. It is thirty years since this photo was taken and my potential is all used up. But these boys are still young.

I've lost touch with the tiger and his brother. Their dad was a drop-dead handsome firefighter, their mother a California beauty. The pirate and his family moved to Japan. He was my son's best friend in preschool; they planned to marry the same girl, Phoebe, and live together in one big house. I don't know where he is now. Phoebe too is an unknown. The boy on the end, with the wide smile and wearing all black, was a wild child. I once came into the kitchen when he was over for a play date and found him on top of our refrigerator. His mom and dad were in the movie business—we used to joke he would end up a stuntman. They moved to a beach town up north and I have no idea what he does now.

I know more about the whereabouts of kids who aren't in the picture, the ones just outside the frame. The unhappy stories are the ones we hear about. A large, stocky boy in a baseball costume was an athlete. He made it to the minor leagues then ended up in rehab. He sells real estate now. The girl hanging around all those boys—dressed as a flapper in high heels at age four—was a tall skinny child. She skipped college and became a model, met a wealthy, much older Hollywood producer who married her when she was twenty and divorced her at twenty-five after three kids. I saw her recently, still beautiful, but a lost look in her eyes and a bitter tone as she spoke to her eldest.

The boy with the crazy hair who stood beside my husband as he took this picture was dressed as Dracula—and not just on Halloween. He was already well aware of the Bella Lugosi movie. Most of the other parents thought it was a mistake to let him watch that kind of film. Thirty years later he's been recently released from jail. He's an addict like Lugosi, but an unsuccessful actor, his brain now so addled and life on the street so debilitating, last time I saw him he was almost unrecognizable. He is not in this picture, but he haunts it, the specter of what can happen to a curly-haired boy.

Each child filled with possibilities. So much promise in each face. Looking at this photo, I cross through the vapor to the past to visit the ghosts of the children they were and the phantom of the young mother I was. I remember how much I hoped for my boy, how much I wanted, and worse, how much I expected.

Halloween is a holiday of desire, of who we wish we were, a chance to wear our inner selves on the outside. A superhero. A ferocious animal. A monster. A little tawdry for those naughty nurse and sexy witch adults, but magical for children. These five boys, all grown—super, ferocious, monstrous, or simply charming—have passed through childhood and stand closer to me. My son, SuperTed, has his own little fairy-winged sprite to take trick-or-treating. His past and his present have taught me to expect nothing from my grandchild, to celebrate only this day and not think about what comes next. It is remarkable she is here. It is enough.

TOD GOLDBERG
CAPITOLA

A few days after my father died, my mom asked me to come over to her house as she wanted to show me something. This was two decades ago, during that brief period when we lived on the same street, like Jews in the Old Country. My mother was already staring down the road at the dead end of life, her existence boiled into a series of doctor's appointments for her cancer, her lupus, and the neurological difficulties that would come into full bloom a few months later, when I would find her wandering naked and lost in her bedroom, incapable of finding her kitchen.

But that was later.

On this day, Mom was sitting in her living room, jazz playing on the stereo, a stack of photo albums beside her, one open on her lap.

This was one of your father's records, she said. He loved jazz.

I knew that much, but precious little else. They'd divorced a year after I was born. Then, for the next thirty years, they never stopped divorcing. Neither had a decent word to say about the other. There were court fights. Warrants for unpaid child support. Years without contact. It wasn't until I was older that I began to consider the very real possibility that they must have loved each other passionately to hate each other so venomously.

Didn't he play the trumpet for a while? I asked.

Saxophone, she said. He was very gifted. Excellent, really. She turned a page in the photo album. He gave it up not long after we were married. It seemed so strange to me at the time. He loved it so much.

I sat down beside her. This reverie wasn't exactly new. A few years before, my mother ran into my father in a grocery store in Palm Springs and an unusual thing happened: They didn't kill each other. They stood in the produce aisle and talked like people who'd once been in love. Let me ask you something, my dad had said, do you still have my old jazz records?

I do, said my mom.

When I was a child, she'd often stand in front of the record player in her bedroom and flip through the records, maybe pull one out, read the liner notes, stuff it back on the shelf. I can see them: John Coltrane, Art Blakey, Kenny Burrell. Those great Blue Note covers from the era. Thing was: She never played them. I wouldn't get to know what they sounded like until I was much older, years after both my father and mother were gone, when I tried to imagine who they'd been.

My mom said, Do you want to come get them? I think I've had them long enough.

No, he told her. He was in town visiting his own father. But I'd sure like to listen to them.

And so, for a few hours, they put down their swords, sat on the floor of my mom's condo and listened to records. They drank coffee, told stories of the life only they remembered, each the holder of each other's youthful secrets and conspiracies. My mom was nineteen when she married my father, who was barely twenty. Sixteen years and four children later, they were done. In photos, they are Camelot. Beautiful and fit, not a hair out of place, my father a TV newsman in San Francisco, my mother a part-time model and socialite. There were black-tie parties. There were famous friends and bold-type mentions in the gossip columns. There was a beach house. Then another. There was a Cadillac. And there were other people in both of their beds. No one walked out on the other person, they both just left, but one of them kept the children. Neither seemed all that interested in raising us, truth be told. The point is, for that one night, the way my mother told it, they were just Jan and Alan again.

The way they were, after all.

My mother slid a photo out of the album. Here it is, she said. What I wanted to show you. This was the last photo of Alan that I took before the divorce. There's so few photos of you and your brother and your father.

There I am, I said.

You weren't even one yet, she said.

No, I said, I mean dad. I look just like him there.

You're a better person, she said. And then: Look at Lee. He looks so sad.

He's just staring at something in the bushes, I said.

No, she said. He was having angina attacks. At ten years old. He hated being with your father. She stopped. Well, no. He loved your father. That *shtunk*. He really did a number on your brother.

Where was this? I asked after a while.

You don't remember?

No, I said.

The beach house. Capitola. We had it for a little while after the divorce, but I guess you were too young. That was where I always felt like a family.

I only remember the photos.

Do you have any with your father?

No, I said.

Do you want this one?

No, I said, you keep it.

You'll get it eventually, she said.

The record came to an end.

Turn it over, she said, if you don't mind.

I got up from the sofa and went to the record player, lifted the needle, turned the record over. Miles Davis. *Birth of Cool.*

Were you into this? I asked.

No, she said. But your dad loved it.

She ran her finger around the edge of the photo. I heard her sigh. You look so happy in this picture, she said.

She slid it back into the album. I wish he'd known you.

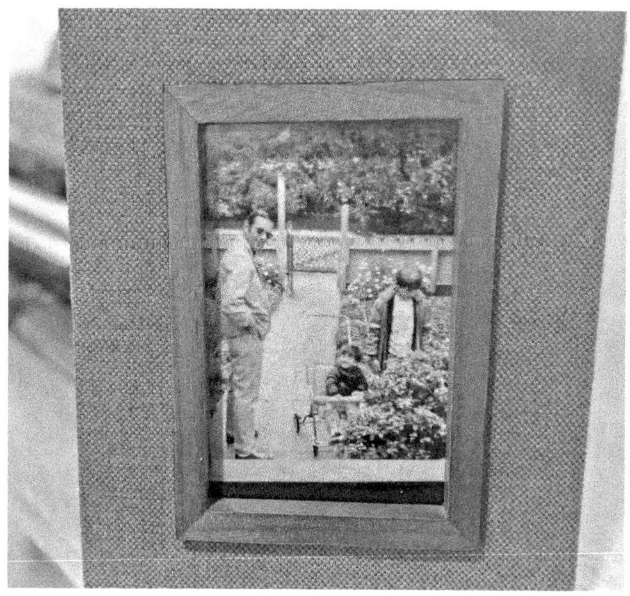

EMILIE PASCALE BECK
HOW TO SAFELY TRANSPORT YOUR WURLITZER

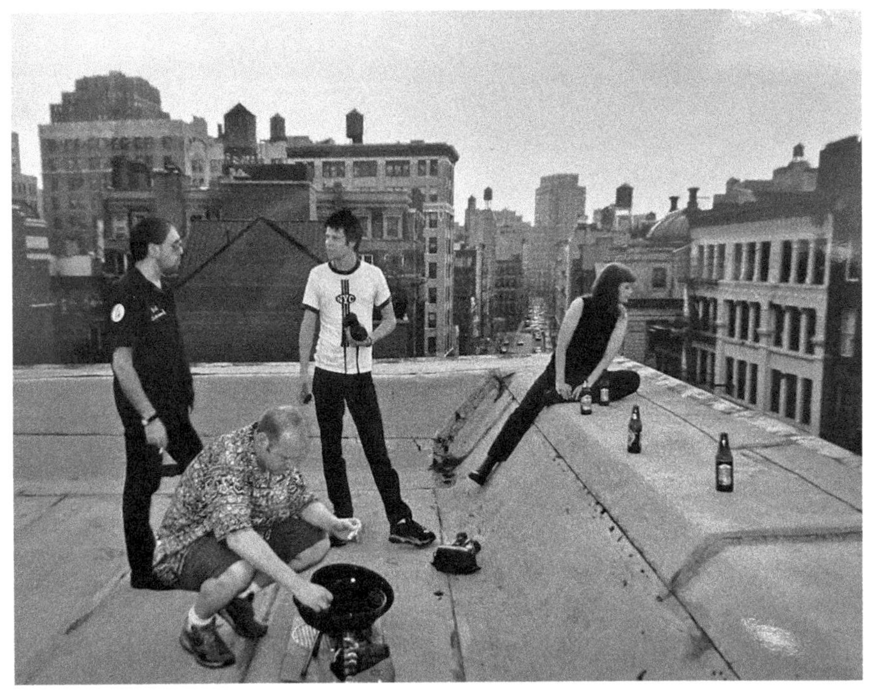

Cordelia was in your apartment below, yowling, yowling. I'd dragged her cross-country to the sixth-floor walk-up in Little Italy, a shower in the kitchen. Access to the rooftop just outside your door. The sunset, that night, was cotton candy. We kept looking and looking away, forgetting, then looking again as it deepened to the inside of a fig, the conversation looping around Y2K, weddings we were going to, music—which shows, which clubs, why WFUV wasn't playing Alan's songs anymore and how you hoped, both of you, that they'd take something from the new album. Alan was one of the few people I knew who would have been good at fame. He'd have somehow basked in it while shunning it. Someone brought the grill up to the roof. Maybe Jimmy and Kathy (Kate, now). Alan made a joke, I'm sure, about my veggie sausage. Dusk settled around us in the shade of a day-old bruise.

The summer was already hot enough that the lady two floors down would sit in front of her door in a bra and skirt, fanning herself. *Che fai*! she'd shout each time we passed. We dragged your futon into the one room in the apartment with an air-conditioner, which was your studio, amps at our heads, the Wurli on my left. When I rolled over, I pushed aside cables with my feet.

Jimmy and Kathy (Kate) had a place in Brooklyn with three cats and Jimmy's vibes. Alan lived on Columbus and 99th in an apartment he still shared with his ex because neither could afford to move out. The walls were lined with LPs. Around 10,000, we later learned. My stuff—cassettes and CDs, books, photos, winter clothing—was mostly packed away in my parents' house in Chicago or the cottage in Los Angeles I had sublet until you and I figured out what we were going to do. Cordelia could have adapted to New York. She'd survived a flat tire in Wyoming, the Loma Prieta quake in San Francisco, and before that, life on the street, which was where I'd found her. In the end, though, you'd had it with the city. You'd been there for twelve years, you said. It seemed like a lifetime.

In LA, you set up your studio in the bedroom, the Wurli in the southwest corner. We put the bed in the dining room, the table in the living room, and pushed the couch up close to the window. Then, when we moved to a house with room for the baby, you used the lower level: a mother-in-law with a separate entrance. Later, when we needed yet another bedroom, we got a place with a converted garage. You covered the walls with huge soundproofing squares.

One winter, several years after we'd left, Alan was moving his record collection a few boxes at a time to a house near the Pennsylvania border, driving there on weekends with his girlfriend, a Broadway publicist of all things. He was happy, which is a funny thing to say about Alan. He and Ruth had bought a place in Sullivan County. They might have been talking about getting married when their car hit a patch of black ice one night, maybe 9 or 10 PM, and they skidded off the road and turned over—the one stretch along that highway without a guard rail.

There was a tribute concert at the Cutting Room. The place was packed. You were on keyboards, Jimmy on vibes. He and Kate had moved up to Woodstock several years earlier. Now they live in a loft in Philly with two gray tabbies and a grand piano that, like yours, was inherited. He uses the large front room as his studio, but she has her own office, four walls and a door. A space that's hers alone. They didn't want kids.

September of that hot summer, almost exactly two years before the towers would come down, we packed a U-Haul, your instruments and equipment carefully tucked between pillows. Streets had been cleared of the San Gennaro Feast but the grease from all those sausages was still underfoot. I don't know how you fit so much stuff into that apartment. (Even now, I wonder at the things neither of us can get rid of—cordial glasses we never use; your monogrammed baby cup, tarnished; the ashes of three cats that I swear I'll plant in a butterfly garden someday.) The truck sagged in the middle and overheated before we got to the Mojave, so we drove the rest of the way with the air off and the windows rolled down. Endless brown hills rusting in hundred-degree temperatures. For most of the trip, two weeks from one end of the country to the other, Cordelia would curl up between us in the front seat, sleeping as we chugged and squeaked through North Carolina, Oklahoma, Texas, but around 8 or 9 PM each night, she'd suddenly stretch her front paws on the dashboard and yowl, as if to say, *Stop! Stop!* And we'd find a motel. Some place to lay our bodies down.

These days, the kids—no longer boys, their bodies lank and sinewy—take over the studio after we've gone to sleep. Drums in the middle of the room, guitars removed from their racks on the wall. They record beats, loops, riffs, vocals. Once in a while, I'll overhear a scratch at a new song. Not anything they're ready to capture, but the first sounds of what might be possible. They'll sit at the Wurli to plunk out notes. Tiny, breathy swells, pulsing, pulsing still, after all this time.

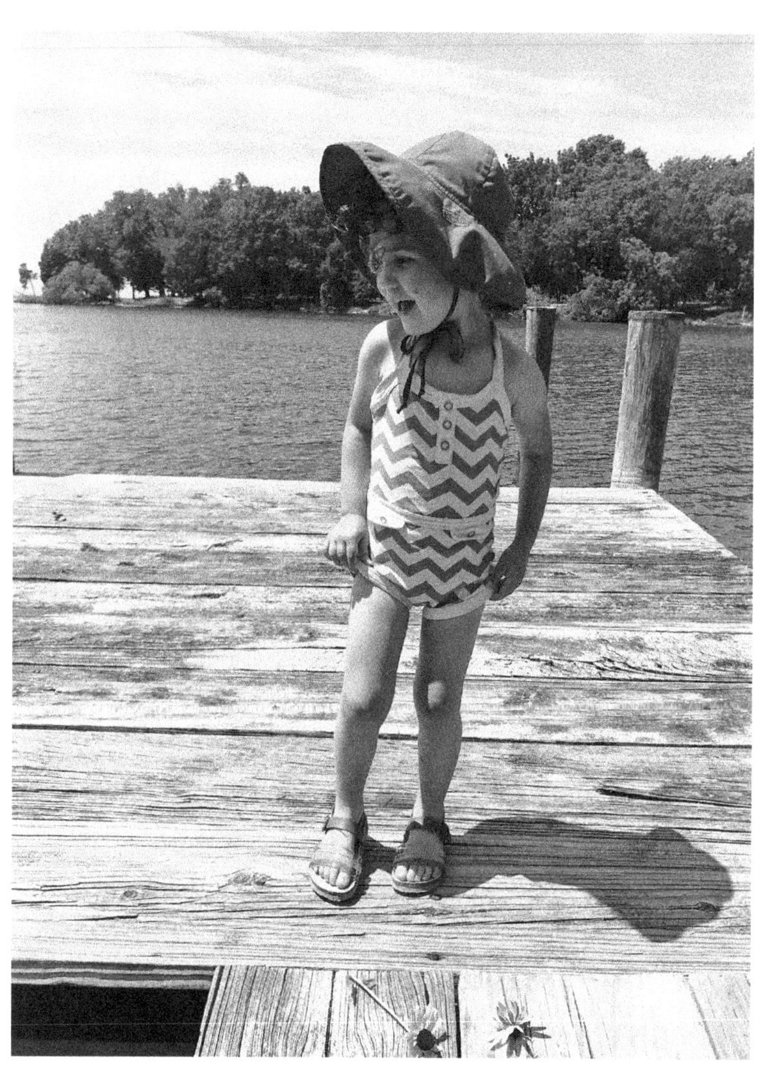

LESLIE JAMISON
JULY 2020
EASTON, MARYLAND

Four months into the pandemic, and this was the first time we'd left Brooklyn: coming down to stay with friends on the Eastern Shore of Maryland. Those Maryland days were full of all the things we'd been missing in the plague city: big skies, big meadows, big sun. Rippling expanses of saltwater. Wildflowers and pancakes. Tiny jellyfish pulsing between the crab boats. We spent hours in a kiddie pool under the blazing sun. We ate ice cream cones by the harbor, counting rusty traps. Joy was so sweet and strange it made our teeth ache; this company—from our friends, from the world—after months alone.

Life back in the city had been life in a ghost town: empty buses rattling down shuttered streets, overflowing hospitals, and chilled warehouses for the bodies; sudden fevers and endless quarantine days. Locked stores with handwritten signs plucked from apocalypse films: *Due to the spread of COVID-19 we are closed indefinitely.* For the first month, it had been me and my daughter quarantined in our tiny apartment perched above an empty coffee shop. This was our coffee shop, our Rom Com set, called Café Regular, and always full of regulars—until the virus arrived, and suddenly all the regulars were elsewhere, shut away like the rest of us. I got sick and then I got better. The virus left her untouched. Finally, I could smell strawberries again.

Once we could leave the apartment, I started pushing her stroller through the empty streets—to the polluted industrial canal, the closest we had to a shore—and, twice a week, to her father's apartment across the park. Three miles there, three miles back. Three miles back with an empty stroller; the ghost-limb tingling of its lightness. We'd signed divorce papers on Valentine's Day, right before the end of the world.

Down here in Maryland, my daughter and I walked on water. Or at least it felt that way to her. And sometimes, honestly, to me. We walked right to the edge of an old dock stretching into the tidal estuary, feeling hot wooden planks under our bare feet, baked by hours of sun. My girl in a sun hat, for once—I almost always forgot. But I'm sure she didn't have sunscreen everywhere she needed it. I've never been a perfect mother like that. I've been a good mother in other ways. I'll get down on the floor and play. I'll track every single word that comes out of her mouth. I'll track the emotional tensions of every imaginary scenario she invents: All the dolls are having a birthday party, but they won't invite the littlest doll to come. Josephine from preschool is getting kidnapped by Hades and taken straight to the underworld. I listen hard. I take it seriously. I'm always making suggestions. She rarely takes them. (*Stay out of my narrative!*) But

I sometimes forget sunscreen, or a water-bottle. I'm not worried enough about a dock without a rail. I never forget the book of fairy tales.

Down in Maryland, my daughter slept until ten in the morning. In a whole pandemic she'd never done a thing like that. In her whole *life* she'd never done a thing like that. Her whole body was exhausted by good things: running barefoot on the grass, against the wind.

Sometimes I looked at her little body—long limbs, round curls—and couldn't believe it had once been tucked entirely inside my own. And neither could she. In her own ways, she was figuring out where my body stopped and hers began. She spent her days finding pairs of objects and naming them: Mama stick and baby stick. Mama pancake and baby pancake. Right there on the dock, by her jelly-strap-sandaled feet: Mama flower and baby flower. These mamas and their babies were separate, but never too far apart. Whenever she looked at a particular photo of me pregnant, from the day before her birth, she said, "Baby in the mama house."

My friends—two women I adored, who'd been married for two years, my daughter had been a baby at their wedding—hosted us in their farmhouse in the fields. (They joked, "We are the lesbian farmers Rush Limbaugh was afraid of.") At night, they fed me fresh-baked cookies and listened to my dating war stories—the banker with a fentanyl problem, the musician with a monogamy problem—and warned me against compromise. It didn't feel like the issue was compromise. It felt like the issue was heterosexuality itself.

Just two weeks later, I'd meet the big love—the one I'd been waiting for, as they say, except that's not exactly right. It wasn't exactly waiting. It was more like working, and learning, and figuring out how to be a person who loved as best she could—without cheating, or drinking, or starving, or cutting, or disappearing at the first sign of trouble—so that by the time I met him, I'd be ready to love a different way.

At that dock, in the sunlight, I had no idea we were at the end of something—with my daughter in her zig-zag one-piece and the daisies at our feet, mama and baby. Mama and baby. This trip marked the end of an era, though I did not know it then: the era between one man and another, when it was just me and my girl, those just-the-two-of-us days, in our treehouse above the coffee shop. For months, of course, it had been a treehouse above an empty coffee shop: no more café regulars, at the Café Regular. No more chain-smoking elderly man flaunting his knowledge of the Napoleonic Wars; no more grad students reading Heidegger and not helping me carry the stroller up the stoop steps. Funny what you miss, once it's gone.

6 ELEGIES

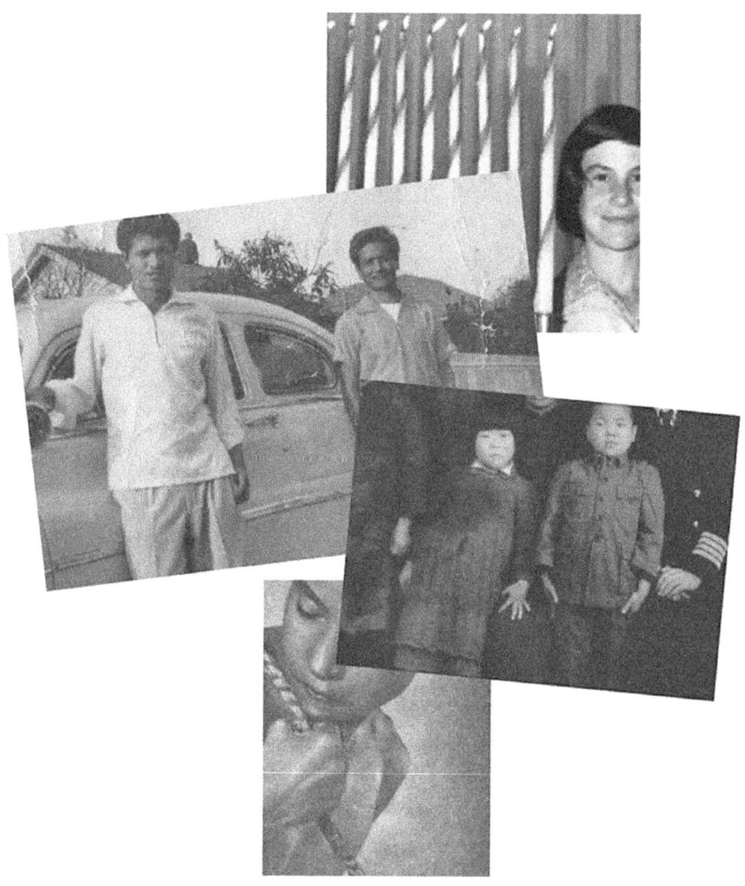

"How dare you, photograph, see him more clearly than I!"

AMY GERSTLER

ALEX ESPINOZA
TAN GUAPOS

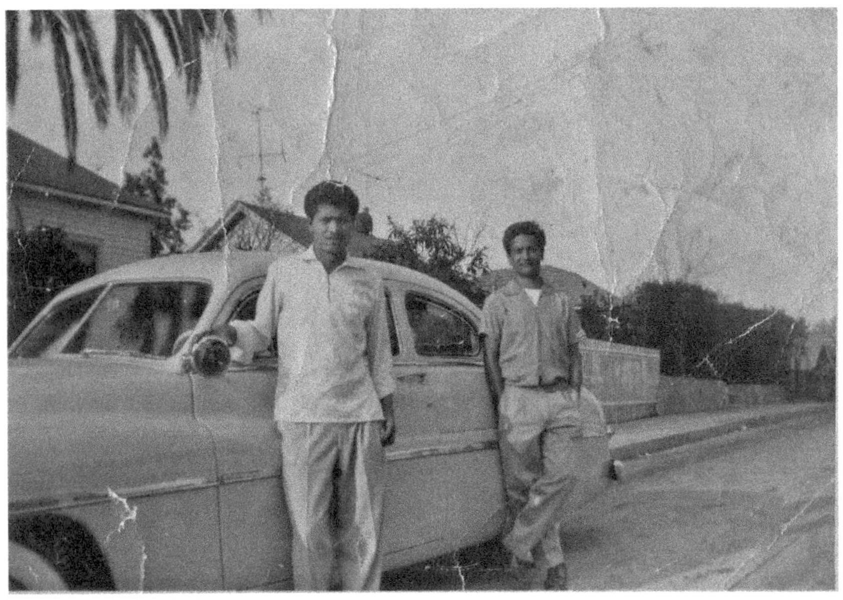

My mother once said it was taken somewhere in Tijuana, but that might have been a lie. Or simply incorrect. Like so much of our history and the history of those dispossessed—all of us immigrants who are uprooted, called away to distant, hostile lands—stories are misremembered, dates changed, names forgotten. So much about us is incomplete. We fill in the gaps with speculations, random guesses. We are our own most puzzling enigmas. It might be a street in San Diego, El Cajon, or the Central Valley, where my father and uncle once worked picking grapes in the fields near Delano, where they lived in a shack with no running water near a polluted stream. And yet she said it with such certainty, pointing to the dirt street, the houses, their fences, the multitude of wires crisscrossing the sky above. She remembered that neighborhood, that palm tree, that man on the roof over her brother's thin shoulder.

"¿Esta segura?" I asked her a long time ago, when I first saw the picture as a kid thumbing through one of our photo albums, the sticky corner of the page yellow and frayed.

"Claro," she replied. "You don't think I remember? I know where this was. Tijuana. I had just arrived from Michoacán with your brothers and sisters. He was surprised and angry at me for coming. I didn't tell him. Someone we knew sent word to them that I was there and they made their way as soon as they could."

"Where were they?" I asked.

She shrugged her shoulders. "Who knows. Besides, what does it matter?"

So, I will say that they're in Tijuana. I will say that my father and my uncle—his brother-in-law—made a pact once the land around el rancho refused to yield anything worth money, once raising pigs to sell was no longer enough to sustain their growing families. They decided to do what all men their age did back then. They packed up what little they had and made the long and complicated journey north. No specific destination in mind. Someone might have mentioned Nueva York, Texas,Florida, or other places in America where relatives or friends or strangers back in El Ojo de Agua might have settled. I will say that this was right after they first arrived. They're both optimistic, and their clothes are pressed and clean. *Tan guapos*, my mother and aunt would say years later. So different from the men they became, how they ended up; both drinking themselves to death. One succumbing to cancer, the other's lifeless body found by the side of some railroad tracks.

I will repeat this story, because it's the only one I have, because it's the version of my father and my uncle—and the countless men like them—that I'm determined to preserve in my memory. It's the look of resilience etched into those two brown faces that most captured my attention when

I first saw this image. My uncle stands with his legs slightly apart, gripping the car's sideview mirror, shoulders back. My father leans against the back door, legs crossed, both hands in his pockets. There's his faint smirk. Even then, his characteristic playfulness, that side of him I never saw growing up, that side my mother swore was once there, is on full display. I want to say that I wish I knew this father and this uncle, this version of them that existed before they were twisted and mangled by the caprices and demands of their new home.

This country complicated them, led them to believe that another life was possible if only they worked hard, if only they struggled and fought and bent to the whims of a nation that relied on their hands and backs, their sweat and sacrifice. So far from home, long distances and time kept them away from their land, their families. I know they went first to Chicago and took jobs wherever they could find them—at meat packing plants, construction sites, textile factories. Without papers, they lived in the shadows and dark corners of that foreign city, evading the police, only talking to others like them.

"Imagine the fear," my mother often said. "Living like that changes you. It's no surprise your father and my brother turned to alcohol."

I try doing that, even now, years after they've both passed on. I try sitting with that fear, try feeling what it must have been like in a place where you know few people and don't speak the language. To experience such confusion and loneliness. I can't tap it, though. I can only summon a thin thread of emotion, weak and transparent as smoke, reaching out to me on random days. Alcohol became their solace, the only warmth they must have had during icy midwestern nights. By the time my mother reunited with my father, after they'd spent years apart, around the time she insisted this photo was taken, he was different, she recounted.

"The Federico I met that day wasn't the same man who left me years before back in Michoacán," she told me. "Your uncle as well."

My father wasn't my father by the time I was born. He was too far gone into his addiction. Too drunk all the time to communicate with me. Same thing with my uncle. I used to resent them both, mocked what I considered their weaknesses and their reliance on substances to numb them. There was so much I thought I understood, but pictures don't always reveal everything. This image always makes me want to reach out, stretch my arms across the distance and time that separates us, tell them to stay strong, to remember that they are loved and will never be forgotten. And that I will do everything in my power to never let this country and its demands swallow me whole.

VANESSA HUA
MEMENTO

When I was putting together a slideshow for our wedding, I asked my parents if we had any old family photos that I could include.

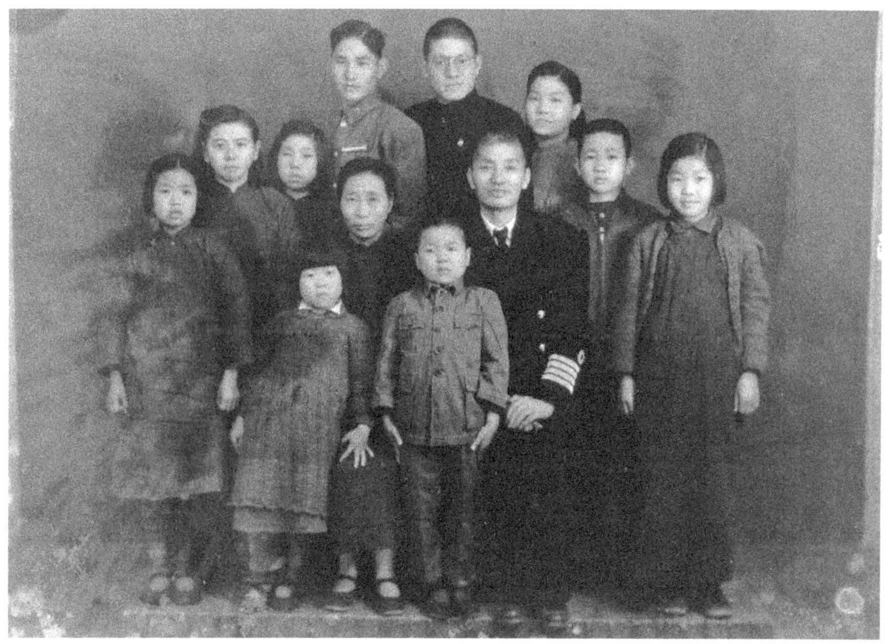

Nanjing, 1947

In this one, out of the dozen people solemnly posed, my father immediately caught my attention.

His familiar stoic expression and large Buddha's ears were the giveaway, the long lobes that signify good fortune. I was 24 years old, and it was the first time I'd ever seen a photo of him as a kid.

The scarcity of documentation of my father's early years imbues this photo with a singular power. I wish I could recall where he dug it up, what he said about it then, or how I felt holding the photo. But I've lost the memory—and my father—in the nineteen years since then.

With programs to print, wedding favors to make, teeth to whiten, a rhumba to practice, scanning the photo was just another task in a long to-do list. My friends were starting to get married and with the advent of cheap, accessible digital cameras and equipment, wedding slide shows were de rigueur.

A typical sequence: black-and-whites of grandparents and parents in the olden times; then the orange-hued Kodachrome snaps from early childhood; then glossies from high school and college, parallel lives until photos of the couple appear on various outdoor and travel adventures, with a pleasing sense of inevitability. At the reception, our slideshow spooled on a screen beside the guest book, yet another requisite prepared but only briefly glanced at that day.

The photo wasn't on display in our house in the suburbs east of San Francisco. My parents spoke rarely about their upbringing: Both were born in China, had lived through war, and fled to Taiwan as the Communists came to power. After receiving graduate school fellowships in science and engineering in the Midwest, they met and married.

They didn't have many mementos from the past. In a single day, we snap more photos of our twins than we have of my father from birth through college. I must have assumed they preferred to focus on the future, rather than dwell on a difficult past. But I realized later that very few photos had been taken during their childhoods. They also might have believed that their tribulations would have been incomprehensible to their three children—a divide not only of generation, but of language and culture, too.

Eight years later, the next time I studied the photo, it was for another slide show: at my father's funeral. Though he'd been ailing from Parkinson's, I thought we still had time—time enough for the questions I'd started asking; time enough for the stories he'd begun to share.

The eulogies revealed a history I'd never known: He bought a diamond engagement ring for my uncle, to propose to his girlfriend. A cousin, newly arrived in the United States, spoke little English, but after learning about Disneyland wanted desperately to go. My father took their family there and even braved Space Mountain; as the car whizzed along the track, he held onto his terrified sister. Another cousin told us from the moment he stepped off the plane with his mother, my father helped them settle in.

And most remarkable of all: My father had used the mysterious family photo to sponsor his parents and siblings for green cards, along with the evidence gathered to prove they were related. I don't know if it swayed the immigration officials, who would have also required other kinds of documentation. But for a family that had been on the run—first from the Japanese, and later the Communists, moving every few weeks from province to province—the photo must have seemed as tangible as anything else my father could have provided.

Roughly a decade has gone by since he's passed away, and I've slowly pieced together more context for the photo, mostly via an aunt, who doesn't speak English. From time to time, I'll text or email questions to her daughters—busy like me with work and family—who in turn ask her, before replying a couple of weeks later. The process is laborious and slow-going, but I'm rewarded with stories that stun me: how they crammed into inns or shacked up with relatives during the war. How my grandmother sold off jewelry to buy food or for bribes for safe passage. How they once fled in a wood-burning truck, in use because of gas shortages.

Recently, I studied the image, noticing new details, or rather, interpreting them anew. They're warmly dressed, perched on a short platform. Was it cold in the photo studio, cold in the city of Nanjing, the country's capital? My aunt has confirmed that the picture was taken during the winter in 1947, when the older siblings—young adults—returned for the holidays. My father lived there several times during his childhood. Within a year, most of the family would leave for Taiwan, just before the Communists overtook the city.

My grandfather, seated beside my grandmother, is distinguished in a tie, with four braids at the cuffs of what could be a military uniform. Most of the brood that surrounds him isn't dressed as formally. My father wears a handknit sweater, as do several other children; the girls are in tunic dresses with leggings and Mary Jane style cloth shoes. Their hair is bobbed; the boys' close-cropped—practical, not fussy.

No one smiles, which lends the scene an antique air, as though from an era when subjects stayed still for long periods of time to avoid blurring the result. The original was spotted in silver, the kind of decay that doesn't happen to digital images, which pristinely and instantly freeze a moment.

Only now do I consider how this might have been one of the last times the family came together as a whole. With so much lost to war and immigration, the photo—and the story behind it—survived when so much else did not.

And, doing the math, I realize my father has to be the same age as my twins, on the cusp of adolescence, when we begin to consider the world more broadly and deeply; when we begin to take steps toward independence. At first glance, their upbringings—my father's, my boys'—couldn't be more different. And yet, they are also familiar with seismic upheaval. At the start of the pandemic, I worried about the impact the turmoil would have on their development. I worry still. But this photo reminds me that in arduous times, my father found a way through, and so too my children now.

AMY GERSTLER
ENVY

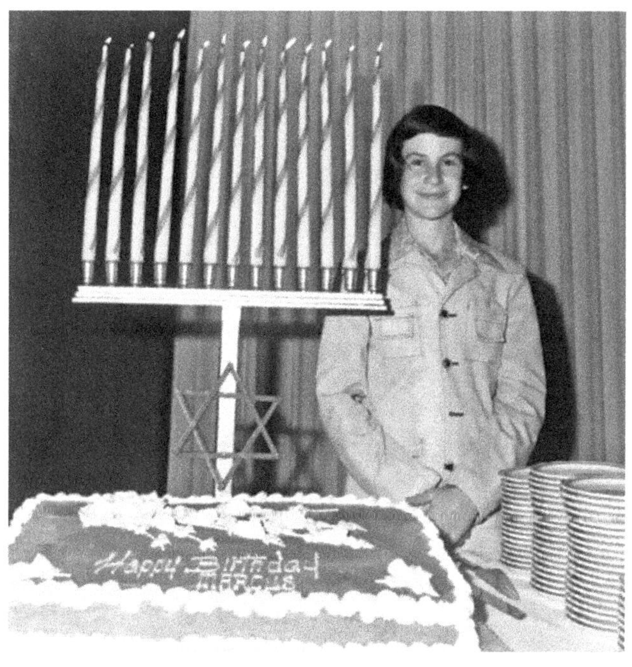

Why my little brother had a Bar Mitzvah, I'm not sure. Our family was not religious. Our parents wouldn't have pressured him or cared. He must have had his own reasons for wanting one. A verbal kid, he loved jokes, puns and new vocabulary words. So it makes sense he might have been eager to learn Hebrew. Also, Marcus (his name's inscribed in icing on the sheet cake in the photo) was, I think, a guy who liked being part of a tribe. He was a joiner. Teams, barbershop quartets, other singing groups, clubs. So maybe he craved Judaism's sense of community. Then there's the music connection. Bar Mitzvahs involve a certain amount of singing. Marc and our mother were avid, talented vocalists. He had perfect pitch. Listening to him was always a pleasure, musically and because his singing seemed part of a general exuberance. And hearing him sing gave that satisfaction which comes from watching someone do something they are fantastic at and seem born to do. Attending my sister's dance performances or gymnastics meets elicited the same reaction.

I must have been present at Marc's Bar Mitzvah, though I don't remember the event at all. Not one moment. I'm seven years older than he was, so I would have had to return from college to watch him perform that rite of young manhood. The original of this Bar Mitzvah photo is in Kodak color, circa 1976. So I know the photo looked old even when it was brand new. Color technology for snapshots back then yielded a muted, limited palette. Blue stripes spiraling around the tall candles are the exact powder blue of Marc's "casual" jacket. The unappetizing brown of the chocolate cake's frosting prints out as the same dull brown as fake wood paneled walls behind the Bar Mitzvah boy. These muddy colors suggest that the past, even when acted out indoors, took place in pervasive dimness. In some perpetual, ill-lit dusk. It's funny, but to me, due to the flat, old timey color, this photo looks more "real," more "natural," in black and white.

How stubborn old photographs are! I mean the ones, like this one, on paper, that you can hold in your hand. Such photos may fade, degrade, and ultimately crumble. Yet as long as they are in decent shape, images remaining legible, then their subjects, their inhabitants so to speak, insist on being fixed, refusing to update themselves, as today's electronic devices are only too happy to do, often without our knowledge or consent. Landscapes, grandmas, dorm rooms, puppies, lakes, babies, cat-shaped birthday cakes, old crushes, swim parties and snow hikes all have lives. They elapse. Yes, the chemicals and paper of old photos are certainly vulnerable. But the subjects in those photos of bygone times (unlike the electronic photos on our phones and computers we can and do mess with) refuse to morph, grow or change as long as the photo retains visual integrity. It's the opposite of the conceit in *The Picture of Dorian Gray.* Oscar Wilde's novel shows us a portrait of a man in which the painted face begins to change, giving physical evidence of that actual man's aging and debauchery. Since old photos don't work that way, they are, to me, both dependable and perverse. Faithful and maddening.

I find I am envious of photos of my brother. Ridiculous, perhaps. But I am not above displacing difficult emotions onto inanimate objects and then blaming them for my feelings. It's often painful for me to look at photos of Marc, not only because he got sick in his early thirties and then died within a couple of years, but because I never got to know him as well as I'd hoped. When I study photos of Marc now, longing, regret, warmth, recognition, tenderness, confusion and something like resentment are all in the mix. As I peer at old photos of my brother, the pictures seem to know him, contain him, reflect and recall him much better than I am capable of doing. And that pisses me off.

Part of the frustrating distance between my beloved brother and me was probably our age difference. I went off to college when I was seventeen and he was ten, so I was out of the house during a key chunk of his growing up. The year before he died, I was driving him to a doctor's appointment and he said, "Aim, I don't really feel like I know you." I was crushed but tried to maintain. Concentrating on navigating the snowy road, I wondered aloud if my intense shyness had created a wall between us. Now that I was forty and had had a ton of—though probably not enough—therapy, maybe we could make up for lost time. I did assure him it wasn't for lack of love or interest that we hadn't been all that close, and that I now wanted us to get to know each other more fully. If we'd had a longer opportunity to grow old together things might have been different. Although my younger self's penchant for wanting to remain mysterious to others, perhaps as a means of self-protection, has lessened but not disappeared. It's only my brother who went missing. Not the list of obstacles and fears that stood between us, known and unknown.

Who are you? I demand of photographs of my brother, including this Bar Mitzvah shot, candles lit, gleaming cake knives and stacked plates ready. *Why are you photos allowed to hold him so staunchly, so doggedly, to keep images of him so accurate that you are ever correcting my incomplete recollections, reducing them to blurred swerves of misremembering, wish fulfillment, and error? Why do you show me up in this way? How is it that you seem to own him, in ways I can't?* These days, in my sixties, I'm trying to grow up a little. It's hard. Attempting to be less of an ingrate, I tell myself that if the photos of my brother are willing to share what they have of him, I had better take what I can get. I sometimes still rail at them: *How dare you, photographs, see him more clearly than I!* But then, remembering who I want to try to be, I add quietly, *thank you, photographs.*

BRANDON SHIMODA
YAMATO

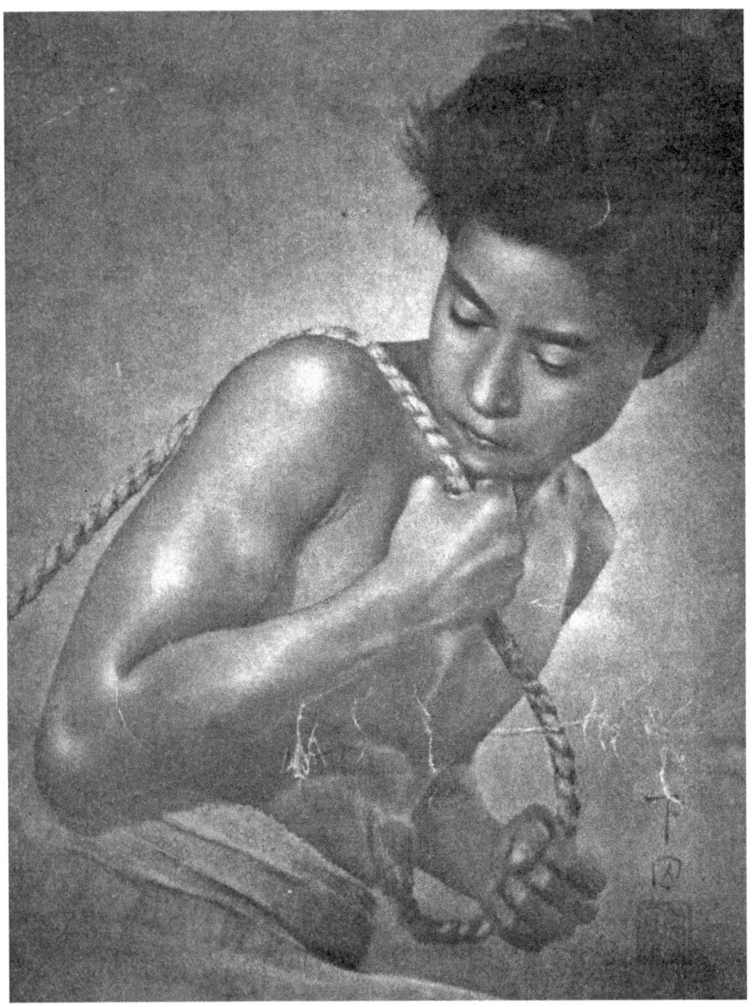

Photo credit: Midori A. Shimoda

What dead do you talk with? That was the first question asked. I was sitting on the stage of a movie theater in Colorado with two artists, Don Christian and Shodekeh Talifero. We had been invited by another artist, Eiko Otake, to talk about talking with the dead, which the three of us agreed—beforehand, on the street—was not something we could, or should, talk about. And yet we'd accepted the invitation. Maybe that is why Eiko invited us: We were the least able, or least wanting, to talk about talking with the dead. (She had just installed a retrospective of her performance work in the museum across the street. In one video, she stared at the camera and said that a close friend of hers just died—she was wearing his jacket.) Eiko sat in the audience, three rows back. We introduced ourselves. Then the moderator asked, *What dead do you talk with?* I thought: I guess we're not wasting any time.

I do not remember what Don and Shodekeh said, not exactly, but how they said it. Beautifully, thoughtfully, but also as if they were starting at the end of the conversation, when the mind has broken free but there is little energy left, or has gone strange. They both talked about family, their mothers and fathers, in a way that made it feel like their mothers and fathers were trapped—in the punishing ways they were living, in the heartbreaking ways they would never live again.

I went last. I was thinking of my grandfather. He was my answer. Almost as soon as my grandfather died (I was a teenager), I started writing about him and have not stopped. I wrote a short story about him in college, then another, which won an award and was published; poems, many poems; essays, even a book. There are many things I've wanted to ask him—about growing up in Hiroshima and Kumamoto, immigrating alone to Seattle, growing up (again) in Seattle and Los Angeles, being a photographer, an enemy alien, a suspected spy—but I have not asked him about any of these things, not really, and not because he is dead. My relationship with my grandfather, which has existed almost entirely in writing, has been less about talking, more about listening. *To attend its voice, I can hear it say, is to embrace its absence*, writes Joy Kogawa, on the first page of *Obasan*, the first book I read about the incarceration of people of Japanese ancestry in North America during the 1940s. But then she writes, *I fail the task*. In truth, I do not want to ask my grandfather anything because I do not want him to feel like he has to say anything. I want to embrace the absence of his voice. That was my answer.

Los Angeles, 1930s. My grandfather had a friend named Yamato. No one knows anything about Yamato. I asked my aunt. She does not know anything. She asked her cousin. She does not know anything either. My grandmother, meanwhile, does not remember Yamato, though she is the one who told me about him. We were looking at a picture my grandfather took of Yamato. It was on my grandmother's dresser—cut out of a magazine, in a small frame. The caption: YAMATO. Attributed to Midori A. Shimoda. *He was Midori's friend*, my grandmother said.

Yamato refers to many things in Japanese history and culture: the people, the province, the dynasty, the clan, the battleship, the poetry, Japan. Yamato, the man in the photo, shirtless, with a cloud of black hair, is pulling something with a rope. He is looking over his shoulder at what he is pulling, which, from the drama of his pose, must be heavy. The moment I said, on the stage of the movie theater, *I want to embrace the absence of his voice*, my grandfather flashed into the darkness. Not as himself, but as Yamato. More specifically, Yamato's right forearm, as it appears in the picture—Yamato's forearm floated in the air. I looked up at it, as if for instruction. I knew it, felt it: its skin, its color, its veins. I missed it, its warmth. I realized—in that feeling, taking leave momentarily from talking about not wanting to talk with the dead—that the picture was not of my grandfather's friend, but of my grandfather—there was no Yamato—and he called it YAMATO.

Why didn't anyone—his daughter, his wife—recognize the man, shirtless, with a cloud of black hair?

Two days ago, my aunt called to tell me that my grandmother has less than a year to live. She called my mom and my sister too. We have no reason not to believe my aunt—my grandmother is nearing 100—but it is hard to tell, talking to my grandmother on the computer, that she is dying or might be dead any minute. She lives alone in a small, antiseptic room in a nursing home far away. She is, in that sense, dying. But she is still present. Recently, I asked her what her secret was for living so long. When she did not respond, I thought maybe she did not hear me. When I asked again, she said, in a way that made it seem like she had been thinking about it for long time and it had just come to mind: *Popcorn and M&M's*. I laughed. She did not even smile. Her white hair was longer than it had ever been.

7 VIEWFINDERS

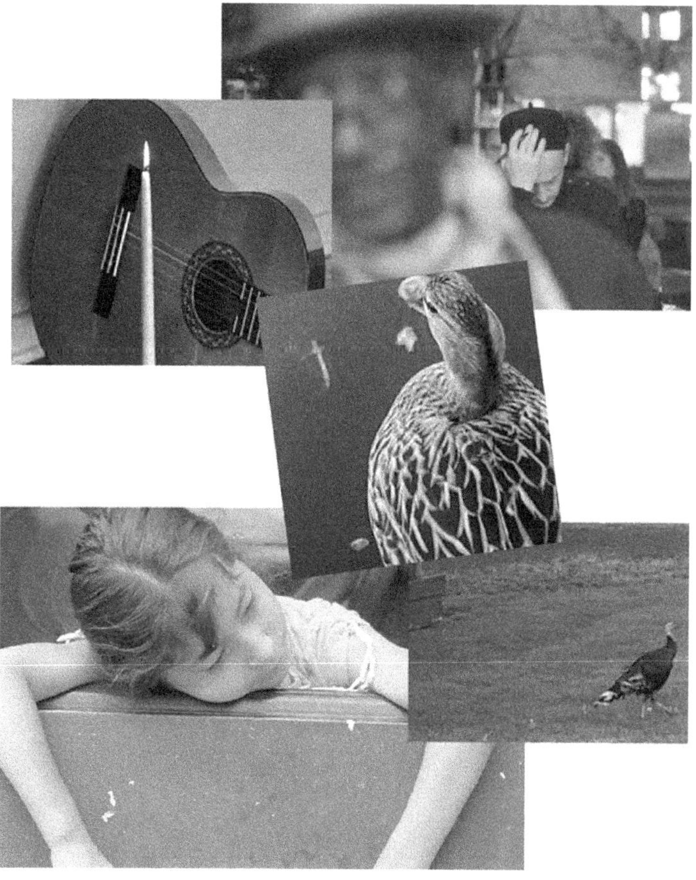

"It is not the girl dreaming of another life, it is the man behind the camera."

DINTY W. MOORE

AIMEE BENDER
GUITAR WITH BURNING CANDLE

The first week's assignment had been people, the second week landscape, and for the third week our photography teacher, lanky, soft-spoken, had asked us to take snapshots of objects. He stood in front of the class in a room that smelled strongly of the chemicals from the darkroom—the hydroquinone, the sodium carbonate, pungent and acidic—the chamber tucked behind a door in the back, where we were learning how to conjure our images from the shining paper. We studied how to modify the light based on how long we left it in the developer, how to lift it carefully with tongs to nestle into the stop bath, and then finally how to dip it for a visit to the fixer. I had needed an elective.

It was 1985 in Los Angeles, and at school dances, "Safety Dance" was still a top hit, and we sang "S, S, S, S," loudly together, spelling out the song. I knew every single lyric of "White Lines" even though I would never try cocaine, even though I often heard mention of parties in the fancy hills where someone was in a bathroom doing lines and the thought of it filled me with terror, as all drugs did, with my aunt having her psychotic episodes, with the simmering anxiety in the home, inside myself. Drugs did not beckon as an exit from that anxiety—they would amplify it, I feared. They would obliterate the tiny bit of self I was grasping onto with clawed fingers. I felt at dances so relieved to have words to sing aloud; it wasn't that I didn't like talking to my friends—I did, I talked to them all the time, hogging the phone, legs up the wall, parsing the minutiae, when it wasn't a minefield of possible digs or sarcasm I couldn't keep up with—but what a relief it was to be on a dance floor with Melle Mel's entire script laid out in my ears and all I had to do was join in.

My mother had found the guitar at a garage sale. Later, I would learn to play it, and with my five chords pound through the folk canon. At this stage, at the moment of this photo opportunity, I had not strummed a note. Whose idea was the candle? Apparently it was mine. And the mirror. The little flame peeking over. When I look at this photo, it reminds me of high school graduation speeches—there is something about cliché when so full and so earnestly employed that I love, that pains and thrills me at once. Oh, adolescence: a guitar I could not play, a taper candle lit in daylight, a carefully angled carpet, everything about it so forgettable and yet I have not forgotten it. In fact, there seem to be several versions from some focused time I spent in that darkroom: a darkened guitar, a washed out guitar. This was my favorite, clearly, because I have an 8 × 11 print in an old scrapbook of high school pictures, including an inexplicable mate photo from the same assignment of the tilted spray of a running shower.

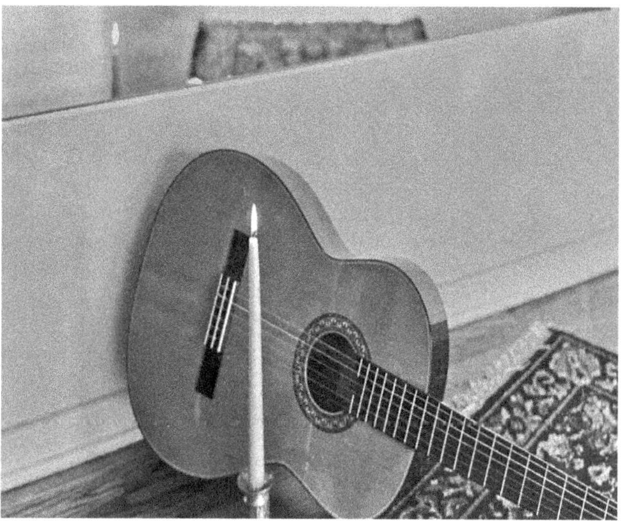

There is a tenderness I feel for that girl, who had buried so much, who did not express, who was quiet, and worried, and spacey, and had she been asked if anything was wrong, would've absolutely said no. I never much liked the class; photography was not my thing. I did not do particularly well, and the teacher took no note of me. Although he retired long ago, it seems the class still exists at this high school, with darkroom and all, even today, and online I found a posting of photos from the 2020 course. Amongst many of the faces, with clever doubling and superimposed images on foreheads, and makeup drawn all over the cheeks, and wild teenage eyeballs, and costumes, and bared teeth, there is one of a solo palm tree, rising high, from the perspective of the base. My heart, my heart.

AISHA SABATINI SLOAN
WHAT'S IN THE BACKGROUND

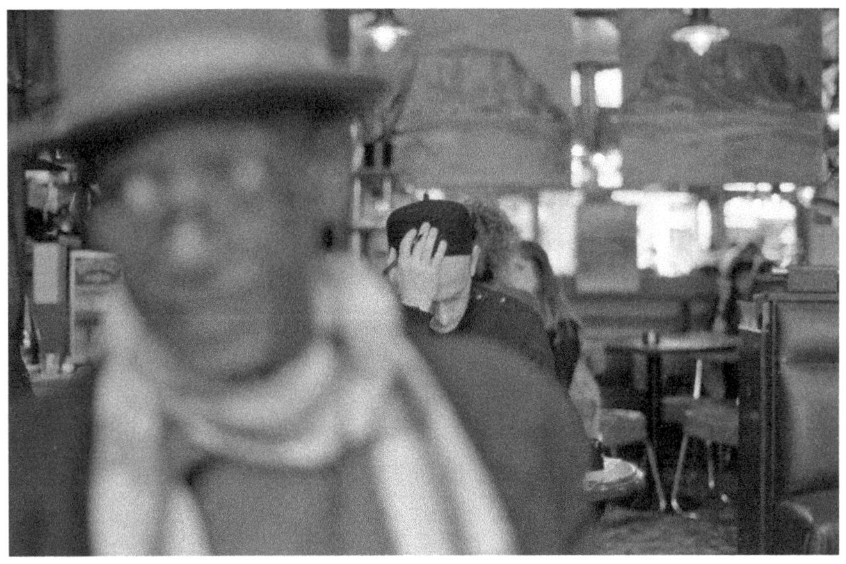

Sometimes I still dream about living in the same space as my parents, in the same reality, the same familial mode. In those dreams and around the block, my father is a blurred version of the person I knew even two years ago. What surprises me is when the haze breaks and the laughter rings out as sharply as it used to. Or when his gaze clarifies and his comic timing is what it always was. I took this picture for the man behind him, his hands. Neither man seemed to want to be studied in this way. It's funny how you can see the eyes of my father's child self, the familiarity of his face now, within the broad strokes of whatever it is, the particular smear and curve of light's absence. John Berger once wrote of Henri Cartier-Bresson, "It's hard to watch his eyes without feeling you're being indelicate. They're totally exposed—not through innocence, but through an addiction to observation. If eyes are the windows onto the soul, his have neither panes nor curtains and he stands in the window frame and you can't see past his gaze." Wandering through Paris, my father used his camera like a superhero's x-ray sight: to peer past the drop cloth in front of him.

When I asked my father to look at this photograph that I took of him twenty years ago in Paris, the following conversation took place. My voice is in bold:

Looks like I'm on the move.

Like you're on the move?

The picture.

I have a whole series where I took pictures with you in the foreground and that guy who was writing behind you in the background because he had such an interesting hat and he kept moving his hand.

I got it.

So when did you learn the technique of pretending to look at one thing while taking a picture of something else?

It's not a technique. It's actually a gamble.

Do people catch you doing it ever?

People respond to the body before they respond to the camera. They see a person standing. If it's a black person the reaction may be different than if it's a white person. They're not looking at what's on your stomach because most people hold the camera up to their eyes when they take a picture.

Mmhmm.

But if you want to take candid—walking down the street, turn around and a guy's walking toward me. You don't lift it to your eyes, a lens, like if you have a wide-angle lens or a 35 mm lens or a 50mm lens. If you have a motorized camera it's even better, you press the shutter and it's going click click click click click.

[Laughs] Do you ever miss the mystery of not knowing what a picture looks like until you get it back from the lab?

No, I have a pretty good idea what it looks like before I get it back from the lab. If it's outside and 125 at f8 or 60 at f11, it's going to be fine. I'm gonna have not one picture but perhaps six if it's a motor drive.

But don't you remember when we were in Paris that summer? We would go, we would bring the film to the lab and then when we would get the negatives back? It was so exciting, it was like opening a present?

You're writing as you talk, aren't you? [Laughs].

I just remember how exciting it was.

It was always fun to see because, first of all, whatever the subject matter it was something you wanted to take a picture of. And then it's exciting as the Dickens when you get it back and you find out they're all in focus or you captured even more than you actually thought you would because of the depth of field and the speed at which the shutter was going off.

But also the composition might show you something that you didn't think you caught.

Usually it's that which is in the background. It's really fun when the person in the background behind the subject sees that you're taking a picture and he or she is reacting and the subject in front is not. Then you've got a dialogue going on, a visual dialogue going on. Because the person in the back looks like he's saying "Hey! He's taking your picture!" You know, mouth is open, something like that, and the person in front is just as cool, no sound has been exchanged, it's just looks. It's a moment, well, it's a moment in time. Those pictures are quite exciting. There's an expression from Cartier Bresson, the "decisive moment." If you take a picture of a guy walking over a pool of water, and then he leaps, and he takes three shots, and one is probably gonna be it.

I like that you talk about Cartier Bresson in the present tense.

Well, he's still alive. He lives through all of us, lives in all of us who want to be like him. Every picture has a history. If you know something about the time, that adds another dimension to what you have, another thing to it, unseen, but to people who know history . . . It's like the woman who owned all of downtown Los Angeles. A black woman. From Georgia or something like that. Denzel Washington made at least two films about Bass Reeves, the first black US Marshal. That's why archives matter—especially those that belong to those who are not of the dominant race, whatever the hell that is. White people weren't here first. Not on the planet or anywhere.

Did you hear that there was a congressional panel recently where members of the military said that they've known about aliens for a long time?

OF COURSE THEY HAVE.

[Laughs]

OF COURSE THEY HAVE. You don't want to scare the hell out of people. The thing about history, it's important to have archives to prove something, or erase it.

So what do you think that this image proves or erases?

The image of what?

The photograph we're talking about.

I've forgotten, which image is that now?

[Laughs] What's your favorite kind of people picture to take?

There's some pictures I shot of graffiti on the walls of some building in Paris, people walking by, and the graffiti says one thing and the image of them says something else. But together they make an interesting picture, they make an interesting statement.

There's people in the picture?

There's people in the picture, a guy and his wife, his girlfriend walking by. And then there's graffiti. Together it's a moment in time. It's the streets of Paris, an everyday scene. It's the juxtaposition of separate moments, but they blend. That's true of life, the way you meet a certain person. Moments in time are just, it's, it's, when everything there in the scene fits. It comes together.

DINAH LENNEY
CATEGORIES

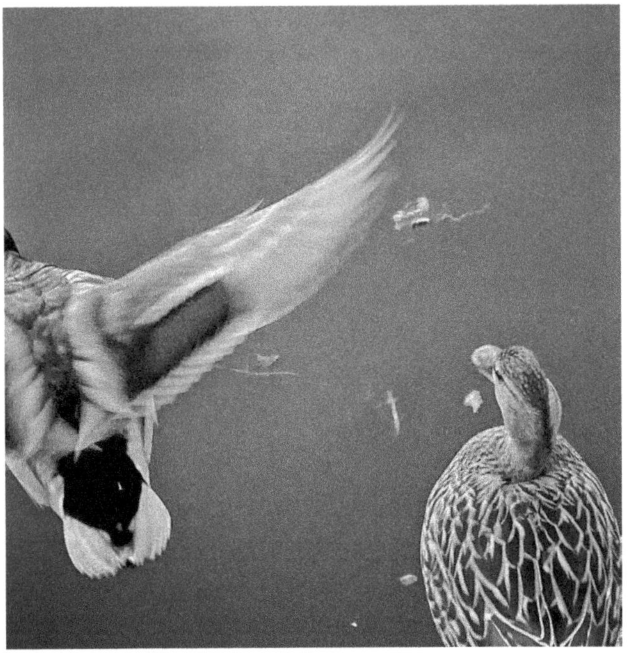

Fair Game

Because picture-worthy: Because how am I supposed to resist the wisteria curling up and over your gutters, or that artful arrangement of terracotta pots, or those big bay windows full of branches and clouds? Anyway, only maybe three times in all these years has a person come out to inquire, politely (and less so—not that I blamed that furious woman, not even at the time), to ask what I thought I was doing, standing in front of their house snap-snapping away. Then up to me to convince them I wasn't looking *in*side, really not. It's the reflection in the glass, I explained each time, the sky, the Jacaranda on the other side of the street, see? Though, if I'm honest, at dusk, lamps lit, I'm drawn past the paned puzzle of purple/green/blue to a vase on a table, or shampoo on the sill, or the pleats in that heavy old curtain, fish in a bowl, perturbable dog, imperturbable cat; most exciting of all, the shadowy profile of a person, oblivious, cooking, gesturing, staring into space.

Pushing My Luck

Because, feigning focus above or below (who am I fooling?), how many pictures have I taken of the guy slope-side at Echo Park Lake, preaching at his congregation of pigeons and geese? And the spectacled reader, tilting back in his chair outside Canyon Coffee most mornings, book and beverage in hand. And how about the little abuela (her broom is taller than she) who daily sweeps the sidewalk outside her little house: How dare I sneak photos of her, much less post them?

And shouldn't I know better than to take pictures of other people's children? I should. I do. My lame-ish defense is I'm careful: I frame from a distance; faces blurred in mid-tag, mid-jump, mid-throw, mid-swing. I guess I shouldn't shoot people unawares. But how to deny myself the thrill of turning my lens on strangers in the throes of real life: smoking, eating (feeding their dogs from the table), drinking, waving, shouting, embracing. I know I should ask, and sometimes I do. But the photos I take with permission, however good-natured my subjects, are never any good. By that time, the moment I longed for has evaporated into that-was-then, instead of this-now.

Once I came home all jazzed about a photo, couldn't wait to show it off—

Walking up the avenue that morning, I'd seen a woman using the payphone a block from the lake, just yards south of Sunset. She was beautiful, dolled up in heels and chiffon, emphatically waving one arm, and didn't I stop to frame and click, and click some more; because the scene so well-played, because we all know those phones don't work, but (very rare) this one had a receiver, a person could pretend, and she did, as if in urgent conversation. She didn't see me, I made sure she didn't, I wouldn't have interrupted her for anything. I was, I supposed, respectful, although—did I bother to investigate why or for whom she performed? I did not. She was bold and I was emboldened. If I thought at all, I thought, *fair game,*

Finally, reluctantly, I started back home; probably I took pictures on my way up the hill (vines, potted plants, bay windows), but the ones of her—at least one of those ones—was the keeper, I knew.

Look at this shot, I said, as I opened the door, handing my husband the phone, scooting around to peer over his shoulder. There she was in banged up stilettos (I'd zoomed in closer than I knew), gripping the handset, stretching the cord as far as it would go, mouth open, eyes closed, as if having a nightmare. Fred shook his head and handed her back to me.

How hadn't I noticed her dress was torn?

The Ones that Get Away

Because I'm not that good.

You'd think I'd give up: You'd think I'd accept that I'll never contain the great whoosh of pigeons at the light at the corner of Fountain and Hillhurst; how they suddenly swoop all at once and then land on the wires—how they do that again and again—and why? Who, which one of them, decides? Whichever, whyever, the frame is too small. The frame is wrong. The frame is the problem! They don't belong in a frame, they will not be framed, never mind this obsession of mine with what? Stopping time? Keeping it going? Can't I take comfort in just having *seen*?

Almost, I can. But to see and realize, damn, that ball is about to bounce over a puddle; that balloon is making an escape; that skipping and skidding umbrella is going to turn itself inside out, where oh where is my phone? And then, never mind, I might say to myself, at least you saw.

What's miffing is to be so determined to see—or to get a worthy photo (they're not one and the same)—that I don't (and I don't). That is, I lose sight of the point, which isn't the picture, not if it's staged, and yet: Don't I, for instance, find myself sneaking up on a Mallard, so bent on getting the shot—those sapphire wings spread wide (blurred, in the end, and half out of frame)—that I miss the actual happening; the flickering, pulsing, tumbling, whirling, sighing, flying—in this case flying!—which, stuck on the duck, I glimpse too late, oh no, look there: a speck of blue heron blurring into blue sky; the life of the present becoming the past before I've had the chance to catch it in the act—

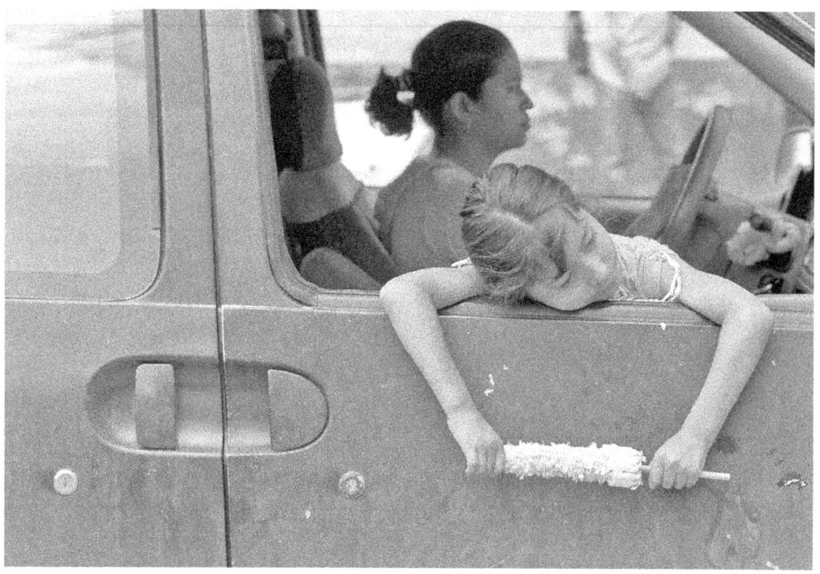

Dolores Hidalgo

DINTY W. MOORE
GIRL WITH CORN

I stood with my back to a small park, on one side of the wide Avenida Sur, in the historic town of Dolores Hidalgo. Intense summer light bleached the facades of the taquerias and the ceramic studio across the way.

I was scanning for something to capture in my lens, when out of the corner of one eye I spotted a girl leaning out of a truck's window, her arms in a triangle, an ear of Mexican street corn oddly resting on the truck's weathered door. Traffic was inching along, giving me just enough time to frame my shot. And by this combination of luck and attention, the picture was born.

Swayed perhaps by the knowledge that Dolores Hidalgo was a starting point of Mexican independence, I soon began to embellish the moment I had captured: The woman in the battered blue pickup has labored most of the day and now drives slowly home, to care for her own family. Her daughter has been rewarded with the ear of street corn for staying quiet and out of the way while her mother worked. The young mother is fierce, determined to make a better life for her child.

Americans visiting countries like Mexico harbor a weakness for romanticizing and invention, confusing poverty for some sign of authenticity. We see Mexican women and children on the street and imagine they are living a more natural and fulfilling life, one of simplicity, rooted in rich cultural traditions.

Such happy people. You can see it in their faces.

But this is purely a product of our yearnings. We are willing to rob these people of their individuality, of their truth, because a certain, simple story offers *us* some sort of necessary comfort.

Perhaps the mother is not determined, but angry. Perhaps she is not the mother but the aunt, unhappy to be sidled with her sister's child once again. Perhaps the girl is dreaming of another life.

*

No, not that either. It is not the girl dreaming of another life, it is the man behind the camera.

It is me.

I have no right to my romantic interpretation—I know none of this, nothing of these two people or their lives.

The temptation to make a story from a simple picture is one of the reasons we love photos, of course. It explains why we imagine so many hidden, suggested, or absent details, and why we convince ourselves that we see what isn't really there. Whether we are in search of artistic images, or simply want to save memories of parties or vacations, we lift our phones and cameras hoping to freeze the moment, to hold time still within the nanosecond where everything fits the story we want to believe. Photographs are fantasies, unreal by definition, because they are static, and reality is not.

The corn is real. The stick holding the corn is real. The truck is real.

The girl with the corn is not at all the story I invented for her. And even if some of what I have imagined were true, it's been ten years since I snapped that image.

For every photograph we see, in our family albums, in a gallery, on our phones, there is the moment after the photograph was taken. And the moment after that. And the following day. And decades later.

The girl with the corn would just now be entering adulthood.

I hope she is doing well.

DAVID L. ULIN
WILD TURKEY

August in Wyoming was hot and shifty. Every time I opened a window, I dislodged a million moths. They were black and rose into the flat sky in a loose cloud that conjured a wraith or demon. Mostly, I kept the windows closed.

In the mornings, I would awaken early, put on shorts and tee shirt, slip outside to walk. South along State Highway 16 to the junction where Highway 14 splintered west like a railroad spur. If I followed that road far enough, I might reach Sheridan. My destinations, however, were more circumscribed. Points of reference, more like, touchstones, stations of a cross of my own making, although I was not undertaking a pilgrimage to Golgotha but rather to myself.

Walking was a path of becoming; I needed it each day to find my shape. So, too, the landscape: I could feel it coalesce as dawn took hold and the sun rose above a field of tall grass where deer leapt through the limpid sunlight and rattlesnakes hid in the undergrowth. I was in Wyoming for a month, on a ranch in the foothills of the Big Horn Mountains. I had not spent much time in such a place. In Los Angeles, I would also rise early to walk, but that was to outflank the morning rush hour traffic. Here, there was no traffic, just the occasional tractor trailer, slipstreaming back and forth as it thundered, at seventy miles per hour, along the two-lane blacktop, transporting heavy construction equipment or bundled bales of hay.

The turkeys clustered in the yard at dusk and daybreak, or maybe that's when I was outside. Chunky and ungainly, they peered from small heads on short necks growing out of bulbous bodies. Sometimes, at the lip of night, they would take flight like lumbering cargo planes, careening low over the lawn in front of the vegetable garden, gaining altitude at the moment before they reached the house. I hadn't seen a turkey fly and it looked like a struggle, as if the effort to remain aloft might be too much. And yet, couldn't the same be said of living? Whatever else turkeys might be, they were also prey, susceptible to coyote, raccoon, bobcat, fox. At night, they nested in cottonwood and spruce. Once, I saw a large adult land on a rooftop, where it plumed its feathers briefly in the rain. Most frequently, I would encounter them while walking, seveneightninetenelevenfourteen, toms and hens and chicks, a blended family, all wandering the gravel shoulder, pecking at the reeds that lined the road.

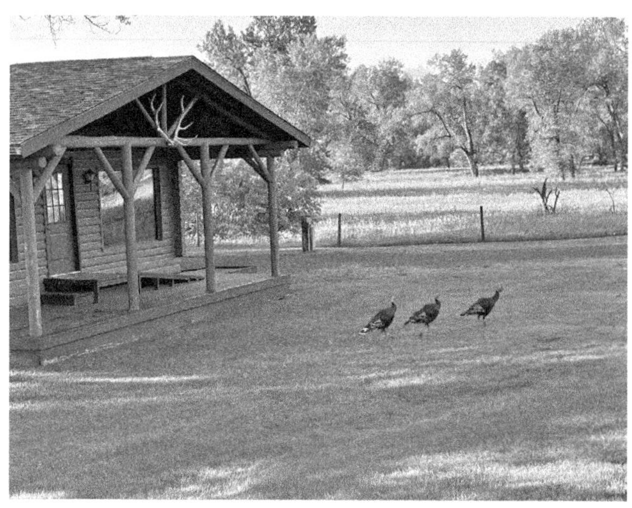

It became an obsession, can I just say that? I couldn't get enough. Previously, wild turkey had been, to me, the name of a Kentucky bourbon. These birds, however, were something else. Pedestrian, on the one hand, so indistinguishable as to seem unremarked. But after I began to pay attention, they were everywhere. Present, or perhaps self-possessed, while also part of something bigger. You might say they belonged. I had never known that satisfaction; I felt, mainly, on the outside peeking in. Certainly, this was how it was in Wyoming. There were so few people, not quite six hundred thousand in a state sprawling ninety-eight thousand square miles, that drivers waved as a matter of course or courtesy as they passed. The turkeys didn't care about that, but they never got run over either, and the only dead turkey I would see had been attacked and then discarded, half-eaten, in the brush.

It felt like a cautionary message about the risk of straying from the flock.

I liked to imagine myself a flock strayer. But the turkeys offered a different sort of context—shared identity, hive mind, small choreographed collaborations, as when, via some hidden stimulus or signal, they would together dash across the road. In the meantime, they continued to cluster, on the shoulder and in the yard but also at the small stone chapel, no bigger than a single-car garage, that had become a terminus point for me. Each day, I would walk there first before doubling back, past the house where I was staying and on, to the ranch road. One morning, in the first light, I noticed on that road what appeared a clot of dried leaves, brown and dusty. I couldn't quite grasp what it was. As I drew closer, the details sharpened: diamond-shaped head, scales, the coiled muscle of a body. I watched it as I slunk away.

Eventually, a friend cut a quill for me from a turkey feather. She gave me a bottle of ink and I bought a pack of canvas boards. I had begun to photograph the turkeys as a matter of daily practice, so I chose an image of three crossing in front of a cabin. *How much do I love these birds?* I wrote, dipping the quill into the ink.

And below it:

These three in particular—
They live here, I am passing through.

The letters came out thick and clotted, as if I'd never held a pen.

And maybe that was the point, maybe I hadn't—not like this in any case. Maybe I was here to fall in or out of something. Maybe I needed to get lost. I thought about those moths, about that coiled snake. I thought about the turkeys in the air. Passing through—that was precisely what I was doing. But sometimes, far from home, in some small corner of the universe, you might meet the unexpected.

Sometimes it might take you down another sort of road.

POSTSCRIPT

ABIGAIL THOMAS
PIGGIES

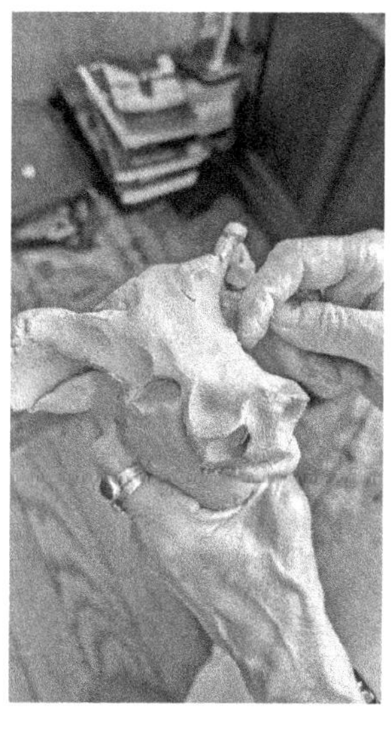

I have in front of me six pigs. Just their faces. They are lined up on the living room radiator which is the only place I had any room. Three of the pigs are pink and one is pink-ish. Of the two darker ones, the one with the ragged ears is black and the other is bright red. I know this because I made them. Each pig stands for a failure.

There are days when the clay is bossy. Maybe bossy is the wrong word. Let's just say I can sit down with a lovely handful, wanting to make a deer, or a tree, or a man reading a book, but the clay has something else in mind. The clay shows me an eye and the broken bones of muzzle or a beak or god knows what and I know I have to find the rest of the face and determine what it was and how it died. Often an apology is called for. "I'm so sorry. We are a rotten species." Or I might be wanting to make a child and the clay wants to be a dog. If I insist on making a child, or trying to, eventually I will have to crumple it up.

After crumpling always comes the pig. Having figured out how to make a snout last March for my sister's birthday, I use these moments of failure to do it again. But only these moments of failure. Otherwise, all I would be making would be pigs, pigs, pigs. You have no idea how satisfying it is to make the snout, pushing a couple of fingers through a thick ball, then pulling them out, making nostrils with a big pinch and oh God you are falling in love again with the beginnings of pig

The booby prize is better than the red ribbon.

ALPHABETICAL TABLE OF CONTENTS

APPENDIX: LIST OF THEMES

The late Judith Kitchen—poet, novelist, essayist, critic, editor, teacher, mastermind (as noted) behind four collections of short literary nonfiction—used to say that readers, not writers, come up with themes. Especially with an anthology, it's the first reader-aka-editor's task and delight to discover overlapping motifs; to eventually land on a structure she hopes will please and pay off. But with shared affinities popping up every which way, how not to acknowledge the possibility of alternate emphases and arrangements? (See introduction . . .) Every essay in this book, wherever it lives, is, of course, informed by memory and the passage of time. But worth identifying, too, are other recurring concerns, strategies, ideas—themes—some of which I've listed below with the names of the writers in whose essays they most obviously surface.

Aging: Emilie Pascale Beck, Suzanne Berne, Sven Birkerts, Amy Gerstler, Tod Goldberg, Vanessa Hua, Ivy Pochoda, Adriana E. Ramirez, Naomi Shihab Nye, Sejal Shah, Brandon Shimoda, Aisha Sabatini Sloan, Grace Talusan, Clifford Thompson, Diana Wagman

Animals and Nature: Emilie Pascale Beck, Stuart Dybek, Pico Iyer, Dinah Lenney, Attica Locke, Naomi Shihab Nye, Abigail Thomas, David L. Ulin

Appetite and Food: Suzanne Berne, Stuart Dybek, Amy Gerstler, Hannah Howard, Wayne Koestenbaum, Alex Marzano-Lesnevich, Sonja Livingston, Ivy Pochoda, Jessica Silvester, Grace Talusan, Clifford Thompson

Arts and Craft: Emilie Pascale Beck, Aimee Bender, Sven Birkerts, Suzanne Berne, Pico Iyer, Major Jackson, Wayne Koestenbaum, Dinah Lenney, Dinty W. Moore, Aisha Sabatini Sloan, Brandon Shimoda, Abigail Thomas, David L. Ulin

Aspiration, Work, Prosperity: Emilie Pascale Beck, Suzanne Berne, Alex Espinoza, Vanessa Hua, Wayne Koestenbaum, Dinty W. Moore, Sejal Shah, Aisha Sabatini Sloan, Susan Straight, Grace Talusan, Clifford Thompson, Diana Wagman

Celebration/Occasion: Suzanne Berne, Sven Birkerts, Amy Gerstler, Sejal Shah, Jessica Silvester, Diana Wagman

Childhood/Youth: Emilie Pascale Beck, Aimee Bender, Amy Gerstler, Tod Goldberg, Kate Carroll De Gutes, Hannah Howard, Vanessa Hua, Leslie Jamison, Sonja Livingston, Aimee Liu, Dinty W. Moore, Naomi Shihab Nye, Ivy Pochoda, Adriana E. Ramirez, Jessica Silvester, Susan Straight, Diana Wagman

Death/Grief: Emilie Pascale Beck, Suzanne Berne, Sven Birkerts, Alex Espinoza, Amy Gerstler, Tod Goldberg, Vanessa Hua, Pico Iyer, Naomi Shihab Nye, Adriana E. Ramirez, Sejal Shah, Brandon Shimoda, Jessica Silvester, Clifford Thompson

Direct Address/Second Person: Emilie Pascale Beck, Major Jackson, Aimee Liu, Alex Marzano-Lesnevich, Sejal Shah

Family: Emilie Pascale Beck, Suzanne Berne, Kate Carroll De Gutes, Alex Espinoza, Amy Gerstler, Tod Goldberg, Hannah Howard, Vanessa Hua, Pico Iyer, Leslie Jamison, Wayne Koestenbaum, Aimee Liu, Sonja Livingston, Attica Locke, Naomi Shihab Nye, Ivy Pochoda, Adriana E. Ramirez, Sejal Shah, Brandon Shimoda, Jessica Silvester, Aisha Sabatini Sloan, Susan Straight, Grace Talusan, Clifford Thompson, Diana Wagman

Friendship: Emilie Pascale Beck, Sven Birkerts, Pico Iyer, Leslie Jamison, Naomi Shihab Nye, Diana Wagman

Gender and Sexuality: Kate Carroll De Gutes, Wayne Koestenbaum, Alex Marzano-Lesnevich

History/Politics/Immigration: Sejal Shah, Vanessa Hua, Brandon Shimoda, Grace Talusan

Identity: Sven Birkerts, Kate Carroll de Gutes, Wayne Koestenbaum, Alex Marzano-Lesnevich, Pico Iyer, Lynell George, David L. Ulin

Luck and Legacy: Emilie Pascale Beck, Suzanne Berne, Alex Espinoza, Vanessa Hua, Wayne Koestenbaum, Naomi Shihab Nye, Sejal Shah, Jessica Silvester, Aisha Sabatini Sloan, Susan Straight, Grace Talusan, Diana Wagman, David L. Ulin

Objects and Metaphor (other than the photos themselves): Aimee Bender, Abigail Thomas, Emilie Pascale Beck, Grace Talusan, Suzanne Berne, Kate Carroll De Gutes, Stuart Dybek, Tod Goldberg, Hannah Howard, Major Jackson, Wayne Koestenbaum, Dinah Lenney, Aimee Liu, Dinty W. Moore, Pico Iyer, Mara Naselli, Naomi Shihab Nye, Ivy Pochoda, Sejal Shah, Jessica Silvester, David L. Ulin, Diana Wagman

Pandemic: Vanessa Hua, Pico Iyer, Leslie Jamison, Wayne Koestenbaum, Attica Locke

Race, Religion, Ethnicity: Alex Espinoza, Vanessa Hua, Dinty W. Moore, Mara Naselli, Adriana E. Ramirez, Sejal Shah, Jessica Silvester, Aisha Sabatini Sloan, Grace Talusan, Brandon Shimoda, Clifford Thompson

Romance: Emilie Beck, Leslie Jamison, Sejal Shah, Alex Marzano-Lesnevich

Travel and Place: Emilie Pascale Beck, Suzanne Berne, Stuart Dybek, Lynell George, Leslie Jamison, Dinty W. Moore, Mara Naselli, Jessica Silvester, Naomi Shihab Nye, David L. Ulin

APPENDIX: LIST OF WRITING PROMPTS

WRITING FROM THE PHOTO AS AN OBJECT

Choose a photo on your desk, night table, refrigerator, wall. Write about:

1. Where it is, in what sort of setting and company; how long has it lived in this spot?
2. If you recently chose to frame it, why? If you framed it long ago, what does it mean to you now?

Choose a photo you yourself took and write about:

1. The moment before.
2. The moment after.
3. Whatever was happening outside the frame.

SHE/HE/THEY IS ME

Choose a photo of yourself:

1. Where are you?
2. Did you take the picture? Why?
3. What do you like about it? What don't you like about it?
4. What do you hope it says about you?

If someone else took the photo:

1. Why did you pose? (Or who caught you unawares? And why?)
2. At the time, how did you feel about the photographer? How do you feel about them now?
3. Is there something or someone in the background that you didn't notice at first?

Do you have a photograph of something—a place, an object—that represents you better than your own likeness?

Write about that.

FROM THE ARCHIVES

Choose a photo of somebody you know (possibly from a time before you knew them), and write about:

1. How the photo does or doesn't do that person justice.
2. How the photo does or doesn't inform your feelings about that person today.
3. A single feature of the subject's face, body, or dress.

With any photograph of any person, known or unknown:

1. What questions do you want to ask the photographer?
2. What questions do you want to ask the subject?
3. What assumptions do you find yourself making about one or the other?

DIRECT ADDRESS

Choose a photograph:

1. Talk to the photographer.
2. Talk to the person or place or object in the frame.
3. Talk to a specific person (friend, confidante) who doesn't know anybody in the photograph or why it's important.

SETTING THE SCENE

Choose a photo of a landscape or vista you love. Write about:

1. Your associations with the place and/or view.
2. The first or last time you visited there.
3. The best or worst memory the image evokes.

Choose a photo of a place where you were a tourist:

1. Why did you (or somebody else) take the picture?
2. Will you ever return?

PICKING AND CHOOSING

Perhaps you're looking at two or three (or more) photos in your possession:

1. What do the images have in common? How do they connect for you?
2. If you were the photographer, what might they reveal about you and your eye?
3. If someone else took them, what pulls you in? What does that say about you and your eye?

MAKING IT UP

Imagine a photo that doesn't exist, but you wish it did. Begin with:
If only somebody [I, you, he, she, they, we] had taken a picture . . .

AND PROMPTS FOR WORKING WITH ANY AND ALL PHOTOGRAPHS

1. What's in the background?
2. What's outside the frame?
3. What does the image tell you about the photographer?
4. Does the photo evoke a story or a memory? Are you surprised to recall something you thought you'd forgotten or didn't know you'd noticed at the time?
5. What do you know now—about the subject, relationships (in and out of the frame), yourself, the world—that you didn't know then?

APPENDIX: A VERY ABBREVIATED LIST OF RECOMMENDED READING

MEMOIR

Homesick, Jennifer Croft
The Years, Annie Ernaux
Still Pictures, Janet Malcolm
Hold Still, Sally Mann
The Rings of Saturn, W. G. Sebald
The Woolgatherers, Patti Smith
A Postcard Memoir, Lawrence Sutin

ESSAY

Camera Lucida, Roland Barthes
About Looking, John Berger
Blind Spot, Teju Cole
The Ongoing Moment, Geoff Dyer
After/Image, Lynell George
Diana and Nikon, Janet Malcolm
On Photography, Susan Sontag

CONVERSATIONS AND HYBRID FORMS

Orphic Paris, Henri Cole
Half in Shade, Judith Kitchen
Talking Pictures, Rudy Burckardt and Simon Pettet
Captioning the Archives, Aisha Sabatini Sloan
This Brilliant Darkness: A Book of Strangers, Jeff Sharlet

ANTHOLOGIES

Brief Encounters: A Collection of Contemporary Nonfiction, Editors: Judith Kitchen and Dinah Lenney
Seeing Things: the small wonders of the world according to writers, artists, and others Editor, Julian Rothenstein, Foreward by Cornelia Parker and texts by Charles Boyle

CONTRIBUTOR BIOS

Emilie Pascale Beck has been published in *Colorado Review, Los Angeles Review of Books, Waxwing, Howlround,* and *LA Stage.* She received the 2022 Levis Prize in Fiction. Also a playwright and director, her productions have won Ovation, Jeff, and Steinberg/ATCA awards.

Aimee Bender is the author of six books of fiction, most recently *The Butterfly Lampshade*, longlisted for the PEN/Jean Stein Award, and her short stories have been published in *Granta, The Paris Review, Tin House* and more. She lives in Los Angeles and teaches creative writing at USC.

Suzanne Berne is the author of five novels, including *A Crime in the Neighborhood,* which won the UK Orange Prize, and a book of nonfiction. Her most recent novel is *The Blue Window.* She lives in Newton, Massachusetts.

Sven Birkerts co-edits the journal *AGNI* at Boston University. He is the author most recently of *Changing the Subject: Art and Attention in the Internet Age*, and *Speak, Memory* in IG Publishing's Bookmarked series. He lives in Amherst, Massachusetts.

Kate Carroll De Gutes is a genderqueer writer whose work examines sexuality and qualities of gender expression in order to explore how butch women dismantle traditional modes of masculinity and inhabit a territory of masculine identity that has nothing to do with cisgender men. As critics have become louder and more oppositional about LGBTQ+ issues, Kate feels an urgent need to counter and subvert traditional images and narratives. Their first book, *Objects in Mirror Are Closer Than They Appear,* won a Lambda Literary Award, the Oregon Book Award, and an Indie's First Award. Their second book began as an experiment on social media, was published as *The Authenticity Experiment: Lessons From the Best and Worst Year of My Life,* and was awarded an Independent Publisher Book Award (IPPY) for LGBTQ+ nonfiction. katecarrolldegutes.com

Stuart Dybek is the author of two books of poetry and six books of fiction including *Ecstatic Cahoots*, a collection of flash-length pieces. His work has been published in numerous magazines including *The New Yorker, Harper's,* and *The Atlantic*, and has been widely anthologized.

Alex Espinoza was born in Tijuana, Mexico to parents from the state of Michoacán. He graduated from the University of California, Riverside, then went on to earn an MFA from UC-Irvine's Program in Writing. His first novel, *Still Water Saints*, was published by Random House in 2007. His second novel, *The Five Acts of Diego León*, was published by Random House in March 2013. Alex's work has appeared in several anthologies and journals. His awards include a 2009 Margaret Bridgeman Fellowship in Fiction to the Bread Loaf Writers' Conference, a 2014 Fellowship in Prose from the National Endowment for the Arts, and a 2014 American Book Award from the Before Columbus Foundation for The Five Acts of Diego León. His latest is *Cruising: An Intimate History of a Radical Pastime* (Unnamed Press, 2019). His newest novel, *The Sons of El Rey*, is forthcoming from Simon and Schuster. Alex teaches at UC Riverside where he serves as the Tomás Rivera Endowed Chair of Creative Writing.

Lynell George is a Los Angeles-based journalist, essayist and author. Her work has appeared in various outlets including *The New York Times*, *Alta Journal, Los Angeles Times*, *Sierra*, and *Oxford American*. Her latest book, *A Handful of Earth, A Handful of Sky: The World of Octavia E. Butler* (Angel City Press) was a 2021 Hugo Award finalist.

Amy Gerstler's most recent book of poems is *Index of Women* (Penguin Random House, 2021). Her work has appeared in a variety of magazines and anthologies, including *The New Yorker* and *The Paris Review*. She is currently collaborating with composer, actor, and arranger Steve Gunderson on a musical. In 2018, she was awarded a Guggenheim Fellowship. In addition to poetry, she also writes fiction, nonfiction, plays, journalism and art criticism.

Tod Goldberg is *The New York Times* bestselling author of fifteen books, including the award-winning *Gangsterland* trilogy; *The Low Desert*, a Southwest Book of the Year; and *Living Dead Girl*, a finalist for the *Los Angeles Times* Book Prize. His nonfiction and shortfiction appears regularly in the *Los Angeles Times, USA Today*, and *Alta* and has been anthologized widely, including in *Best American Essays* and *Best American Mystery & Suspense.* He lives in Indio, CA and is a Professor of Fiction at UC Riverside, where he founded and directs the MFA in Creative Writing & Writing for the Performing Arts. His latest book, *Gangsters Don't Die*, is out now.

Hannah Howard is the author of the number one Amazon bestselling memoirs *Feast: True Love in and out of the Kitchen* and *Plenty: A Memoir of Food and Family*, and the Editor-in-Chief at Parent.com. Her writing has been featured in *New York Magazine*, the *Guardian*, *Bon Appetit*, *Saveur*, *VICE*, *SELF*, *Wine Enthusiast*, *Salon*, and the *Chicago Review of Books*. She teaches writing classes and lives in Frenchtown, NJ with her family. She loves stinky cheese.

Vanessa Hua is the author of the national bestsellers *A River of* Stars and *Forbidden City*, as well as *Deceit and Other Possibilities*, a *New York Times* Editors Pick. A National Endowment for the Arts Literature Fellow, she has also received a Rona Jaffe Foundation Writers' Award, the Asian/Pacific American Award for Literature, a Steinbeck Fellowship in Creative Writing, and a de Groot Foundation Writer of Note grant, as well as awards from the Society of Professional Journalists, the Asian American Journalists Association, among others. A former longtime columnist for the *San Francisco Chronicle*, her work has appeared in publications including *The New York Times*, *Washington Post*, and *The Atlantic*. She teaches at the Warren Wilson MFA Program and elsewhere. The daughter of Chinese immigrants, she lives in the San Francisco Bay Area with her family.

Pico Iyer is the author of sixteen books of fiction and nonfiction, translated into twenty-three languages, on subjects ranging from the Cuban revolution and the XIVth Dalai Lama to our global swirl and the art of stillness. His most recent book, *The Half Known Life*, explores the idea of paradise as it comes to us in often difficult places, from Iran and North Korea to Jerusalem, Kashmir, Ladakh and Varanasi.

Wayne Koestenbaum has published over twenty books of poetry, criticism, and fiction, including *The Queen's Throat* (nominated for a National Book Critics Circle Award). His piano/vocal record, *Lounge Act,* was released by Ugly Duckling Presse Records; he has given musical performances of his improvisatory *Sprechstimme* soliloquies at the Hammer Museum, The Kitchen, REDCAT, Centre Pompidou, Walker Art Center, The Artist's Institute, the Renaissance Society, and The Poetry Project. His feature-length film, *The Collective,* premiered at UnionDocs

(New York) in 2021. He has received a Guggenheim Fellowship in Poetry, an American Academy of Arts and Letters Award in Literature, and a Whiting Award. Yale's Beinecke Rare Book and Manuscript Library acquired his literary archive. He is a Distinguished Professor of English, French, and Comparative Literature at the CUNY Graduate Center.

Major Jackson is the author of six books of poetry, most recently *Razzle Dazzle: New & Selected Poems*. Major Jackson lives in Nashville, Tennessee where he is the Gertrude Conaway Vanderbilt Chair in the Humanities at Vanderbilt University. He is an elected member of the American Academy of Arts & Sciences.

Leslie Jamison is the *New York Times* bestselling author of *Splinters, The Empathy Exams, The Recovering, Make it Scream, Make it Burn*, and a novel, *The Gin Closet*. She teaches at Columbia University, and lives in Brooklyn with her family.

Dinah Lenney is an actor and a teacher and the author of three memoirs, *Bigger than Life, The Object Parade,* and most recently *Coffee,* which doubles as an Object Lesson in Bloomsbury's critically acclaimed series. She co-authored *Acting for Young Actors* with Mary Lou Belli, and co-edited *Brief Encounters: A Collection of Contemporary Nonfiction* with Judith Kitchen. She lives with her husband in Los Angeles.

Alex Marzano-Lesnevich is the author of *THE FACT OF A BODY: A Murder and a Memoir*, which received a Lambda Literary Award, the Chautauqua Prize, the Grand Prix des Lectrices Elle, the Prix des Libraires du Quebec, and the Prix France Inter-JDD. It has been translated into eleven languages and is in development with HBO. A 2023 United States Artist fellow, and the Rogers Chair in Creative Nonfiction at the University of British Columbia in Vancouver, Marzano-Lesnevich's next book is *Both and Neither*, a transgender and transgenre look at the life beyond the binary.

Aimee Liu is the author of four novels, most recently *Glorious Boy,* as well as the memoirs *Gaining* and *Solitaire* and numerous other nonfiction works. Her books have received a Literary Guild Super Release and Barnes & Noble Discover Great New Writers Award and have been translated into more than a dozen languages. Aimee earned her MFA at Bennington College and taught for many years in Goddard College's MFA in Creative Writing Program.

Sonja Livingston is the author of four books of nonfiction, including *Ghostbread*, a memoir of childhood poverty which has been widely adopted for classroom use. She's also written a collection of prompts, *52 Snapshots*, which helps writers jumpstart their memoir projects. Her essays appear widely in literary journals and magazines. Honors include an AWP book prize, New York State Arts Fellowship, an *Iowa Review* Award, an *Arts & Letters* Prize and a VanderMey Nonfiction Prize. Sonja is an associate professor of creative writing at Virginia Commonwealth University.

Attica Locke is a *New York Times* bestselling author of five novels. *Heaven, My Home*, sequel to the Edgar Award-winning *Bluebird, Bluebird*; *Pleasantville*, winner of the Harper Lee Prize for Legal Fiction and long-listed for the Bailey's Prize for Women's Fiction; *The Cutting Season*, winner of the Ernest Gaines Award for Literary Excellence; and her debut *Black Water Rising*, which was nominated for an Edgar Award, an NAACP Image Award, as well as a *Los Angeles Times* Book Prize, and was short-listed for the Women's Prize for Fiction. A former fellow at the Sundance Institute's Feature Filmmaker's Lab, Locke is also a screenwriter and TV producer, with credits that include *Empire, When They See Us* and the Emmy-nominated *Little Fires Everywhere,* for which she won an NAACP Image award for television writing. She co-created and executive produced an adaptation of her sister Tembi Locke's memoir *From Scratch: A Memoir of Love, Sicily, and Finding Home* for Netflix, which was a top ten hit in over fifty countries during its first weeks on air. A native of Houston, Texas, Attica lives in Los Angeles, California, with her husband and daughter.

Dinty W. Moore is author of the memoirs *Between Panic & Desire* and *To Hell with It,* and the writing guides *Crafting the Personal Essay* and *The Mindful Writer,* among other books. He has published essays and stories in *Harper's, The New York Times Magazine, Georgia Review, Kenyon Review,* and elsewhere. He founded *Brevity,* a magazine of flash literary nonfiction, in 1997.

Mara Naselli is a writer and editor. She is a 2014 recipient of the Rona Jaffe Foundation Writers Award and her most recent work has appeared in *Agni, The Believer,* and elsewhere. She lives in Michigan with her family.

Palestinian-American writer, editor and educator **Naomi Shihab Nye** grew up in St. Louis, Jerusalem, and San Antonio, Texas, where she continues to live. She has been Young People's Poet Laureate for the US (Poetry Foundation), poetry editor for *The New York Times Magazine*, and *The Texas Observer*, and a visiting writer in hundreds of schools and communities all over the world. Her books include *Everything Comes Next*, *The Tiny Journalist*, *Voices in the Air*, *Sitti's Secrets*, *Habibi*, *This Same Sky*, and *The Tree is Older than You Are: Poems & Paintings from Mexico*. Her volume *19 Varieties of Gazelle: Poems of the Middle East*, was a finalist for the National Book Award. *The Turtle of Oman* and *The Turtle of Michigan* have both been part of the Little Read program, North Carolina. She received Lifetime Achievement Awards from The Texas Institute of Letters and the National Book Critics Circle.

Ivy Pochoda is the author of the novels *Sing Her Down, These Women, Wonder Valley, Visitation Street,* and *The Art of Disappearing.* Her writing has appeared in *The New York Times, Los Angeles Times,* as well as many other publications. She teaches creative writing at the University of California, Riverside Palm Desert as well as at the Skid Row History Museum.

Adriana E. Ramirez is a Mexican-Colombian-American writer, critic, and poet based in Pittsburgh. She won the inaugural PEN/Fusion Emerging Writers Prize in 2015 for her novella-length work of nonfiction, *Dead Boys* (Little A, 2016). Her reviews, essays, and poems have also appeared in *The Atlantic*, the *Los Angeles Times*, the *Boston Globe*, ESPN's *The Undefeated*, *Los Angeles Review of Books*, *Guernica/PEN America*, and *Literary Hub* among others. She occasionally writes book reviews for *People Magazine*. Ramírez works a columnist and editor of InReview for the *Pittsburgh Post-Gazette*. Her debut full-length work of nonfiction, *The Violence*, is forthcoming from Scribner. She once lost terribly on Jeopardy!

Sejal Shah is a writer, interdisciplinary artist, and teacher of writing. Her debut essay collection, *This Is One Way to Dance* (University of Georgia Press), was an NPR Best Book of 2020 and named in over thirty most-anticipated or best-of lists including *Lit Hub*, the *Los Angeles Times* and *PEN America*. Her debut story collection, *How to Make Your Mother Cry: Fictions* (West Virginia University Press, 2024), is a book about women and girls making their way through a world that excuses the bad behavior of men—a genre-bending text woven with poems, drawings, letters, and black-and-white photographs. More at www.sejal-shah.com and on IG and Twitter @SejalShahWrites. The recipient of a New York Foundation for the Arts Fellowship in fiction, she lives in Rochester, New York.

Brandon Shimoda is the author of several books of poetry and prose, including *The Grave on the Wall* (City Lights, 2019), which received the PEN Open Book Award, and *Hydra Medusa* (Nightboat Books, 2023).

Jessica Silvester is a contributing editor at *New York* magazine's The Strategist and a former editor at *O, The Oprah Magazine.* Her work has appeared in those publications as well as others including *The New York Times* and *Condé Nast Traveler.* She has appeared on *The Today Show* and *Good Day New York.* She earned an MFA in nonfiction from the Bennington Writing Seminars.

Aisha Sabatini Sloan writes about swimming pools, road trips, Jean-Michel Basquiat's obsession with *Gray's Anatomy*, glaciers, and the anxiety of seeking chiropractic treatment. She writes through the fractured lens of art, film, tv, and pop culture. She is the recipient of a 2017 CLMP Firecracker award, the 1913 Book Prize, a 2020 National Endowment for the Arts fellowship in creative writing, a 2021 National Magazine Award for Columns and Commentary, a 2022 Lambda Literary Award for Bisexual Nonfiction, and the 2022 Jean Córdova Award for Lesbian/Queer Nonfiction.

Susan Straight has published nine novels, most recently *Mecca*, and a memoir, *In the Country of Women.* She has won the Edgar Award for Best Mystery Story, The Lannan Prize for Fiction, the Robert Kirsch Award for Lifetime Achievement by the *Los Angeles Times* Book Prizes, and an O Henry Prize. She lives in Riverside, California, with her family.

Grace Talusan is the author of *The Body Papers,* which won the Restless Books Prize for New Immigrant Writing and the Massachusetts Book Award in Nonfiction. Her writing has been supported by the NEA, the Fulbright, US Artists, the Brother Thomas Fund, and the Massachusetts Cultural Council. She teaches in the Nonfiction Writing Program at Brown University.

Abigail Thomas has written three works of fiction and four memoirs, among which are *Safekeeping; A Three Dog Life; What Comes Next and How To Like It*; and her new one, *Still Life At Eighty: The Next Interesting Thing.* She has four children, twelve grandchildren, one great grandchild, and a high school education.

Clifford Thompson's books include *What It Is: Race, Family, and One Thinking Black Man's Blues* (2019), which *Time* magazine called one of the "most anticipated" books of the season, and the graphic novel *Big Man and the Little Men* (2022), which he wrote and illustrated. His essays and reviews have appeared in *The Washington Post*, *The Wall Street Journal*, *The Village Voice*, *Best American Essays*, and *The Threepenny Review*, among other places. Thompson teaches creative nonfiction at Sarah Lawrence College and the Bennington Writing Seminars. A painter, he is a member of Blue Mountain Gallery in New York City. He was born and raised in Washington, DC, attended Oberlin College, and lives with his wife in Brooklyn, where they raised their two kids.

David L. Ulin is the author or editor of nearly twenty books, including the novel *Thirteen Question Method* and *Sidewalking: Coming to Terms with Los Angeles*, which was shortlisted for the PEN/Diamonstein-Spielvogel Award for the Art of the Essay. He is a professor of English at the University of Southern California, where he edits the journal *Air/Light*.

Diana Wagman is the author of six novels. Her second, *Spontaneous*, won the 2001 PEN West Award for Fiction. Her fourth, *The Care & Feeding of Exotic Pets*, was a Barnes & Noble Discover Choice. She has had short stories and essays published in literary journals and anthologies and is an occasional contributor to the *Los Angeles Times*.

PHOTO CREDITS

Unless otherwise noted, all photographs come from the writers' personal archives, and have been reproduced with their permission.